NEVER GIVE UP:

Triumphing Over Polio

A Personal Memoir by Myrna Nielson Thacker

MYRNA THACKER

Lulu Publishing Services rev. date: 03/12/2020

Editors:

Kelley Thacker Ewell, Niece
Randall Thacker, Son
Susan Myers

DEDICATION

To our wonderful mother, sister, aunt, cousin
and friend, Myrna Nielson Thacker.

Thank you for a brave life well lived. Your perserverance,
positive attitude, and humor taught us how to live
a full life despite the trials we may face.

To her parents, Merrill Nielson and Doris Miller Nielson, and the many
family and friends who through their tremendous love, provided an
environment and community of support that facilitated her recovery.

CONTENTS

ACKNOWLEDGEMENTS

Myrna kept detailed journals of her polio experience which developed into a habit of regular journaling throughout her life. We are blessed to have a couple dozen volumes of journals written by her for which she gave us approval to read. Her comment was, "There's not much in there of any interest. You'll get bored reading it." We disagree. We have found her writing to be so authentic and inspiring.

Myrna's children would like to thank Kelley Thacker Ewell, Myrna's niece, who spent countless hours on the phone asking the curious questions that led to the further development of this excellent memoir. All who read it will be forever grateful. Kelley, your phone meetings with Myrna were always something she looked forward to and thoroughly enjoyed. Thank you for taking such a genuine interest in her life and loving her as you did.

Merrilee Thacker
Bryan Thacker
Randall Thacker

CHAPTER I

A Life Changed

I was an energetic and full of life 14-year-old, the only remaining child living at home with my parents, Doris and Merrill Nielson, in Spanish Fork, Utah. My oldest brother Kent had left home to join the Merchant Marines and subsequently married and settled in Portland, Oregon. My other brother, Gordon, was serving active duty on the front lines in the Korean War.

It was a beautiful Sunday in November. It had snowed all of Saturday, the ground was covered with snow, and the trees were frosted in white. The winter of 1951-52 was one of the heaviest snow years in Utah history, and we in Spanish Fork had gotten our share of the bounty.

Our home in Spanish Fork with lots of snow

My parents and I had gone to Salt Lake City over Thanksgiving weekend. It was our family's tradition to go there and spend it with my Uncle Ralph and Aunt Phyllis, or Aunt Erma and Uncle Jake. We'd always go shopping on Friday and part of Saturday and it was a big deal. It wasn't like now, where people buy clothes any time of the year.

Spanish Fork had a JC Penney's, but everyone shopped there, and we wanted to go someplace different so we weren't wearing the same clothes as everyone else. Mother always said that if you bought clothes at JC Penney's, you'd see yourself on every corner. In Salt Lake City, we'd go to ZCMI, Auerbach's and the Paris, which were the big department stores at the time. Auerbach's was on the corner, and then we'd cross the street and go into Kress's and come out onto Main Street and walk up to ZCMI. Before we'd get to ZCMI, there was Greyson's, and in its window on this trip was the coat of my dreams. It was lavender, with a light-yellow scarf and gloves, and I fell in love with it.

Downtown Salt Lake City circa 1951

My father would drop us off and then drive away between the buildings, through an alley-way, and park in a lot somewhere. Sometimes, he'd go have a piece of pie, or do some shopping of his own, but other times, he'd go visit with my Aunt Erma, or other family. I was never quite sure what he did while mom and I were shopping, but it always amazed me how he knew every time just when and where to come and pick us up.

We returned home Saturday evening and I was really looking forward to wearing my new coat to church the next morning. I woke up that

Sunday morning wanting to hurry and get ready for church so I could wear my new coat. I was like any young girl who is excited to show off her new clothes. As I started to get out of bed, I noticed that whenever I talked, laughed or even yawned, my chest hurt, but I shrugged it off, attributing it to all the shopping and running around we'd done the days before in the cold.

Church was fun as many of my girlfriends had new clothes too. I received enough compliments about my new coat that I was smiling very happily to myself until I saw a girl in church who was wearing the exact same coat as me. We'd gone all that way to find something a little out of the ordinary, and there she was, wearing my coat! I felt better about the situation by reminding myself that this girl was much older and always very well-dressed.

My dad was the United States Forest Ranger in Spanish Fork. When we arrived home, his former assistant, Grant Williams, was there with his wife, Hope. They visited with us and Grant took a colored photograph of the three of us in our bright coats—Dad's red wool dress coat, Mother's maroon winter coat, and of course, my lavender coat with its puffy sleeves at the shoulders. I could just imagine how the picture would turn out.

After dinner, Mother let me go over to my friend Janet Gardner's to play in the snow. Even if we were young ladies just turned fourteen, it was still fun. Lois came over after a while, and then we decided it'd be even more fun if we could go get Doris. She lived too far away to just run over, and because all afternoon my chest had been getting more and more stiff, I didn't really want to go. But Janet and Lois wheedled and coaxed me into it, and Mother took us down. We had a lot of fun building a snowman and throwing snow at each other.

On Monday, my chest still hurt. Mother wondered if it could be pleurisy because Uncle Ralph had it when we were there for Thanksgiving. Pleurisy is an inflammation of the membrane that lines the chest cavity. Mom must not have thought it could be serious or she wouldn't have let me go to school. On the way to school, walking along with Janet, I mentioned to her that my toes were numb. I thought they were just cold, because all winter it had been very chilly. At school, I told all my friends about the pleurisy, but none of them had ever heard of it. They thought I was just feeding them a line, and wanted to know what the joke was.

That night after supper, Janet and I went to the movie, "Behave Yourself," at the theater. I remember that it was very unusual to go to a show on a school night, and so it was quite an occasion. I don't remember just why my parents allowed me to go, but maybe something was allowing me a little bit of extra freedom before I lost it so completely.

Spanish Fork's Movie Theater circa 1950

The next morning, I got up at quarter to seven, like I always did, to practice the piano. The stiffness in my chest had turned into a backache, and while I practiced I needed to keep leaning on the piano to hold myself up. Mother gave me a worried frown, and said that I had better stay home from school that day, but I didn't want to. I was captain of our basketball team, and I needed to buy some ribbon for the girls on my team. We would tie the ribbon around our wrists, and the opposing team would tie ribbons of another color around theirs so we could tell our teams apart. I want to make it perfectly clear that I was only captain of the team because the coach had drawn our positions out of a hat, and not because of an extraordinary talent for playing basketball.

Mother didn't look very happy to let me go, but I could see she wasn't sure if she should be all-out worried yet, so she didn't argue with me. She gave me an aspirin and told me to take it after I got to school. I did, but the aspirin didn't help, and the ache in my back only got worse. Civics was quite boring, as always, and so I noticed my backache more than I would have otherwise. But when I went down the hall to math, I didn't have time to think about it. When the bell rang for lunch, the pain was back with a vengeance, raging up and down my back, so I gave Donetta Burrows the money for the ribbon and asked her to get it for me.

Mrs. Jensen, the gym teacher, asked Anne Banks to walk home with me, and she made me run the whole way home. All afternoon I lay on a hot pad, but nothing seemed to help.

After school, my friend Barbara Banks came down to see me and keep me company. After she left to go home the pain seemed even worse. Mother had that worried frown on her face again.

"Let's take your temperature," she said.

"I wouldn't have a temperature with just a backache," I replied.

"We will take it, anyway," she said.

She did, and the thermometer registered 100 degrees. I couldn't believe it. I knew my back hurt, but the thought of having a temperature, too, hadn't even crossed my mind. The worried frown on Mother's face deepened. The pain in my back only worsened, so I went to bed. Janet came in for a few minutes to visit. When she left, I turned on the radio to keep my mind off the ache in my back. After supper, which I couldn't touch, Mother took my temperature again and it was up to 101, so she phoned the doctor. He was there by seven-thirty.

"It couldn't be polio, could it?" she asked him.

"No, I don't think so, these aren't the symptoms you get with polio. She probably just has the flu in her back. I'll give you a prescription and you can get it filled."

"Will it help in a hurry?" I wanted to know. I couldn't believe how much my back hurt, I wanted to cry it hurt so much. The doctor smiled at me, and promised it would work in less than fifteen minutes.

As soon as the doctor left, Mother went uptown to get his prescription filled. It seemed to me as if she was gone forever. The pain was so bad, and the waiting for relief was so hard. By the time she finally came home, and I had taken the pills, it was nearly nine-fifteen. Half an hour later Daddy came home from painting classrooms at the church. The pills still hadn't helped. Daddy took one look at me, and got that worried frown on his face. He gave me one of his sleeping pills, but it was just like drinking a plain glass of water. The pill had no effect. My temperature was still climbing, and had now reached 102. Mother phoned the doctor again, and he said to double my pills. This we did, but it only made me vomit, because by then I'd taken so many.

The pain grew worse, and by two-thirty a.m. it was unbearable. Mother called the doctor again, and this time he said to put me in a tub of very hot water. This finally eased the pain, and after getting out and drying off, I was able to sleep for about fifteen minutes. Then the pain was back, gnawing and gnawing, with never any relief. I ran some more hot water, climbed back in, and again this just relieved me for a moment. Mother phoned the doctor, and he said to try hot blankets. Daddy went downstairs and put some blankets in the washer with hot water, then put them through the wringer and brought them upstairs in a basket, damp and steaming. Mom wrapped them around me on the kitchen table where I was lying so I could stretch out. This helped, too, but again, only for a little while.

All this time I couldn't bear to keep still, I could only stand the pain by constantly moving. First, I'd lie on the floor, then walk back and forth, and even run and jump. Maybe something in me knew this would be my last chance to move like I wanted. Daddy even offered to rock me in his arms if I thought that would help, but nothing helped for very long.

Through the night, I snatched only fifteen or twenty minutes of rest here and there, and when I woke up Mother or Daddy was always by my side, watching over me. I thought then that I had the most wonderful parents in the world. At six a.m. the next morning, Mother phoned the doctor again, and he told her to take me to the hospital. It was the Wednesday after Thanksgiving.

At 10 o'clock I walked into the hospital, and the doctor gave me a hypodermic shot and a pill. I finally found relief. I fell asleep in a hospital bed and woke up at different times of the day, only to be given another hypodermic shot and a pill. I slept the day away in blessed relief.

Sometime during that dreamless twilight of waking and returning to sleep, I heard a woman crying outside my doorway in the hall. It sounded like Mother to me, and when she came in a while later, I asked her why she had been crying. She said no, no, it wasn't her, it was some other poor woman, but I found out later that it had been her crying. The doctor had told her that I had polio.

Later that night I tried to eat something, but it all came back up. About 9 o'clock I felt like I had to go to the restroom. I wanted to get up and walk, but Daddy wouldn't let me. I felt like I just had to see if I could walk. I guess subconsciously I already knew that I had polio. The nurse put me on the bedpan, instead.

My legs started to hurt, and daddy rubbed them with alcohol. I also noticed that I had a hard time turning over. At midnight Mother came, and Daddy went home. All night long mother helped me turn over when I got tired of lying on one side or another. I could feel my legs getting weaker and weaker. As dawn approached, mother went home, saying that she'd be back soon. The nurse brought me some orange juice, and I sipped it while I waited for mother to return.

Mother came in at about 9:30, all dressed up, and said, "We're taking you to Salt Lake."

"I've got polio!" I cried. "I don't want to go to the hospital in Salt Lake!"

"It'll only be for a few days. We're getting President Wallace Gardner to come and give you a priesthood blessing." President Gardner was a good neighbor, and a local ecclesiastical leader of The Church of Jesus Christ of Latter-Day Saints.

"Why?" I cried, "Do they think I'm going to die?" I didn't really think that I was going to die. I wasn't sure why I said that. I guess I was just fishing for some reassurance that I would be fine, that it was all a mistake, and that I didn't really have polio.

Just then Daddy and President Gardner came in, and he gave me a wonderful blessing. I can't remember what he said, but I will never forget the feeling that came over me. It was a warm, loving and peaceful feeling. I knew that things would be fine. The entire time President Gardner was praying, Mother, Daddy and I had tears flowing down our faces. Then the doctor and Daddy carried me out to the car.

CHAPTER 2

Into Isolation

Daddy settled me in and put my suitcase in the trunk while Mother tucked blankets and pillows around me. I lay down on the back seat and Mother sat beside me and helped me sip 7-UP all the way there. Our doctor in Spanish Fork had said that he would call ahead and tell them we were coming.

We were almost to Salt Lake City when we were pulled over for speeding. Daddy told the policeman that he was taking his daughter into Salt Lake because she had polio, and had to go to the hospital there. The policeman immediately told Daddy he would escort us the rest of the way to the hospital.

The Salt Lake County Hospital was located on the corner of 2100 South and State Street. I'll never forget when we turned onto the street of the hospital. The sight was very familiar to me, because it was the road we had always turned on to go to Uncle Ralph's and Aunt Phyllis's house, and to the home of Aunt Erma and Uncle Jake.

I thought about how much I loved my aunts and uncles. Aunt Phyllis was small and shapely, always fashionably dressed. She used henna on her hair to make it a little brighter red. Back then, no one colored their hair. She and Uncle Ralph were always so generous, hospitable and really the only ones in the family who had any money, as Uncle Ralph was a banker. Aunt Erma was warm and welcoming although of modest means and had gray hair, with a faint tint of blue, a common thing that older women did to their gray hair.

We went around to the back of the hospital, where an orderly waited with a stretcher. The reality of my illness was beginning to sink in. He took me through the halls and into a little room. Not long after that an intern came in. He asked me to lift my head, and I was proud that I could. Then he got me a paper cup with a straw in it and had me blow bubbles so they could check my lung capacity and see whether I had the kind of polio that affected my breathing. Then Dr. Thomason came in and repeated the whole performance. The doctors told me they'd need to take a spinal tap to see if what I had was truly polio. "What else could it be?" I asked. The reply was that it could be any number of things.

The doctors asked Mother and Daddy to leave the room. The first doctor held me in a fetal position so that Dr. Thomason could get the needle between the vertebrae and into the actual spinal cord and draw some of the fluid into the needle. He showed me the needle before he inserted it, and it was just like any other hypodermic needle. He joked and talked to me while he was getting the fluid, and it didn't seem so bad. Yet, when he turned away with it after drawing it out of my back, he showed it to me. I saw that he'd actually used another needle, and it was quite a bit bigger, thick and jagged, with teeth at the top. The first needle had been to anesthetize the area where he was going to insert the second needle. I understood why he hadn't shown me the second needle before he'd drawn the fluid, because I would have been scared. By examining the fluid, the doctors determined that I did, unfortunately, have polio.

There were three types of polio: spinal, bulbar (which affected the throat muscles), and respiratory (which affected the lungs). I had spinal polio. I was mostly paralyzed from the waist down. Fortunately, four years after I got polio, in 1955, Dr. Salk developed a polio vaccine. It was made from the dead virus, and was welcomed with cheering from the children, and weeping on the part of many of their parents. A Dr. Sabin was working from another angle. He thought the dead virus would prove to not be as effective, and was working with an attenuated, or weakened, virus. His vaccine came out soon after, and both were used to keep people from getting polio.

The doctors put me on another stretcher, and the nurse took me over to the children's polio ward. It was believed that polio was contagious, so all polio patients were put into isolation until they were basically well, and all chance of contagion was gone. My symptoms were like having the flu, but by the time I was let out of isolation, polio had left its calling card.

I was put in a big room that had only two beds. The other bed was empty, and I was the only one in the room. The nurse took everything I owned and gave it to Mother, and then she dressed me in a white nightgown. Mother left after a little while, the nurse went to tend to other patients, and I was left alone.

All that day I suffered, and the only thing the nurse would give me for the pain was a little white pill. The doctors wanted to follow the natural progress of the illness, and if I'd been given pain relievers to the point of relaxing my muscles, it would have masked the symptoms of it progressing into my lungs. The nurse kept bringing me juice to drink, and insisting that I do so. The juice made me gag, it was so sweet it was sickening, and it kept coming back up, leaving a bitter burning taste in my throat. The vomit got all over my sheets, and in my long hair. I would call for the nurse to come help me. Sometimes it seemed like an eternity before someone would come to my aid.

I couldn't turn myself at all by now. I was so uncomfortable, first on one side, and then on the other, that I kept calling the nurses. There was no way to buzz for the nurse to come help me, I could only call, "Nurse! Nurse!" I'm sure they thought that I was an annoying patient.

At midnight, the nurse started to put hot-packs on my legs and body to relieve the pain. That was the first time I felt relief. Up until then everything had been hard and painful, and this was the first time I felt I was receiving care that made a difference. I would drift to sleep, throw off the hot-packs, and call for Daddy.

Everything had happened so quickly and had been so hectic, there hadn't been a quiet moment to reflect that there was someone else who could help me. Then I remembered about prayer. Suddenly, it hit me that I couldn't kneel to pray, so I lay there on my back, folded my arms, and said a silent prayer. That is the position in which I've said my morning and night prayers for the remainder of my life.

In the hospital, everything was so immediate and draining that the pain and sickness, and not being able to see my parents, became the focal point in my life. But even through all that, I still had implicit trust in God. Looking back, I don't know how I would have gotten through the next three years without that faith. I know God was there for me then, and I know that God has been there for me in the years since, as I've gone on to face different and sometimes harder challenges. I'm so grateful that my parents taught me, when I was very young, about prayer and our Father in Heaven and the Savior, Jesus Christ.

Later, it nearly broke my heart when I found out that Mother and Daddy would only be allowed to visit me on Tuesdays, Thursdays, and Sundays. Even then just one could come, and they could stay for only fifteen minutes. When they visited me, they were dressed in white gowns, with paper slippers on their feet and masks over their mouths. They weren't even allowed to touch me.

The next morning, a Dr. Judge introduced himself as my doctor. I asked him how long he thought I'd have to be in the hospital, and if I would get to go home for the holidays? He sadly told me that I wouldn't be home for Christmas—I would still be lying flat.

Friday came, and the nurse took me to another room and constantly kept the hot-packs on me. That night Mother and Daddy sent me a letter and a comic book. I tried to read both, but my eyes were so weak from the polio that the words were just a blur.

For some reason, I had this idea that someone in the hospital was supposed to be wan and pale, but somehow also pretty, in a fragile way, so I combed my hair, tied it with a ribbon, and even put on lipstick. I must have gotten the notion from the movies where every woman in the hospital had perfect hair and make-up. I don't know why I even bothered because I was so sick, and I felt so awful.

By Sunday I felt a lot better. I could hardly wait until 2 o'clock came so that Mother would come. When she did, I started to cry with relief and pity for myself. I'd missed her so much, and I missed Daddy too. I was so scared, and I still didn't feel better. I didn't know what having polio would mean for me, and in a lot of ways I was still a little girl who needed her Mother very much. The time came, all too soon, when the nurse told Mother she would have to go, and I cried some more. I was just too tired and sick, and scared, to even try to put a good face on it. I could tell that Mother felt awful, too, at having to leave me, but there was nothing she could do about it.

I was so lonely after she'd gone. Tuesday seemed so far away. One of the nurses must've felt bad for me, because she was so nice. She suggested that my parents get an old radio for me. It should be old, she said, because I'd have to leave it when I left the hospital. So, about 10:00 o'clock that night Mother and Daddy brought one to the hospital. My Aunt Phyllis had fixed up an old one and given it to them to bring to me. She'd even painted it yellow, a nice cheery color. That old radio sure saved me, and helped to while away the long hours. Every morning on the news they would announce how many more people had come down with polio, so I felt that I'd been in the news. I swear that it was that year, the winter of '51, that the song "Frosty the Snow-Man" came out, because I'd never heard it before.

Every morning the radio played a program, "My True Story." Mostly they were love stories. One day when Mr. Eastman, the physical therapist, came in, I was listening to the program, and he started to work on my legs. After a while I asked him if he wanted me to turn it off, but he just shushed me up. He was as interested in it as I was.

The radio helped pass the time on Monday and Tuesday while I waited impatiently for Mother to come. Daddy let Mother come, even though he might have said it was his turn, because he knew how much she wanted to see me. By then I could go four hours between hot-packs. I was slowly improving.

After mother left that night, the nurse took me to another room that had two little boys and two girls in it. There were screens between the boys and the girls for privacy. They all had only mild cases of polio, and they could still run around. They would throw clay, and some of it would get in my hair. That may have been another reason I was such an ornery patient. Then the nurses took us all down the hall, where we watched cartoons on a screen they'd set up for us. The other kids had fun, laughing at Woody Woodpecker and Porky Pig, but it didn't interest me. I was a lot older than the other kids, the cartoons were boring, lying on the stretcher was uncomfortable, and I hurt so much. I was miserable and I just didn't want to even be there.

On the brighter side, I received quite a bit of mail from my friends, which was wonderful. It was so nice to know that so many people were thinking about me and cared so much about me. On Sunday, my cousins Kathy, Linda, and Julie sent me a plant, and every night Mother and Daddy brought a letter to the hospital, but I still couldn't see them except during visiting days.

For some reason, I could never sleep very much during the night. The nurse would close the door so that there was just a two-inch crack, and the only thing I could see through the opening was the light from a burning bulb in the ceiling. That light became very comforting to me. I've since learned how important light is in so many ways. Light can lift your spirits, light shows you the way, and I think that at the time, it gave me something to focus on instead of the pain.

The night nurse would get quite angry with me for bothering her so often to come in and turn me again. I decided that I'd need to learn to turn myself, so I pulled on the edge of the bed until I managed to get myself over, but I could only do it when I was wrapped from my waist down in hot-packs. I could roll myself over like a log when my legs were wrapped together as one.

Finally, on Wednesday night, the nurse brought me chopped foods. It seemed good to be able to eat real food again. Thursday afternoon Daddy came to visit, and I started to cry, as usual. I asked him if he thought it would be possible for me to go home for Christmas. The thought of staying in the hospital was too disheartening. He said, "We'll make it out for Christmas. You just see, we'll make it. We're also going to try and get you up to the LDS Hospital." The allure of the LDS Hospital was that I'd be out of isolation, and Mother and Daddy could come and see me any day they wanted.

Eventually, some other girls shared my room, but they went home, and I longed to go home, too. The only thing that made it even remotely bearable was that my homeroom class at school sent me a beautiful bouquet of flowers, so I knew they were thinking about me.

That night, in the dark, I got to thinking about what Daddy had said. "If you don't see another day of school this year, you'll be promoted up to high school anyway." I replied that I would surely be in school by March, at the latest. He thought so, too. It all would depend on my mobility.

The day after I entered the hospital the physical therapists started working on me. The purpose of therapy was to start stretching my muscles. Polio had caused them to tighten up. For them to even lift my leg up off the bed was painful. The therapists would move every group of muscles in my legs for me in all the ways that they should normally be able to move. They would stretch my muscles by pushing just a little past what was comfortable for me.

At first, I thought the therapists would get me up on my feet and start me off walking, but I couldn't move a thing below my waist except my left foot and my right big toe, and I could push my right foot to the right. One of the common misconceptions about polio is that because your muscles are paralyzed, you must not be able to feel anything, but this wasn't so. Polio could destroy the nerves completely, only partially, or just weaken them.

Saturday morning, I listened to the programs on the radio and ate an orange that one of the nurses gave me. It was rotten, and I couldn't figure out if she knew it was, and gave it to me because she didn't like me, or what!

On Sunday I put my hair up for Mother because I wanted to look nice for her, but by the time she came, it had sweated out because of the hot-packs. She asked me what she could bring for me, and I told her that some gum and mints would be good, since I'd found out that it would be fine for me to have some. The next time she came, she brought some, and they sure did taste good and helped relieve my boredom.

I told Mother that the night before, Dr. Thomason had come in and told me that when she and Daddy had first brought me in, he and the other doctors had thought that I'd be paralyzed all over. He'd made the remark that a lot of people must have been praying for me to have gotten better as much as I had. Mother said they had been, and that they still were praying that I could get completely well and come home. He also told me there'd been an iron lung outside the door since I'd first been admitted to the hospital, as I'd had all the indications of needing one. At first I thought he was just trying to make me feel good that I hadn't needed it, yet I remembered that first Sunday morning when this all started how it had hurt to yawn or laugh.

Examples of iron lungs used by polio patients

The iron lung was a great big tank six feet long on legs, open at one end. The nurse would slide a patient in, feet-first, on a stretcher, and the whole body would be enclosed, except for the head, which stuck out and rested on a little shelf. A mirror hung above the head so the person could see around a bit. The iron lung helped a patient to breathe by pumping all the air from the tank, thus creating a vacuum, causing the chest to rise, and take in a breath. Then the lung would fill up with air and push the chest down, causing the person to exhale. The pump moved the air from fifteen to thirty times a minute. Without it, patients would have suffocated, because their lungs couldn't move on their own.

On Monday, Dr. Thomason came in and talked to me. I enjoyed talking with him because he was always so encouraging and upbeat. He talked to me about how he'd always wanted to be a specialist, and that it had taken him nine years of schooling and a lot of hard work to do it. He said that during that time he could have given up, and stayed as a general practitioner, but he wanted to specialize in his field. He told me not to quit until I was where I really wanted to be in life. This conversation inspired me in the days and years to come.

Days in a hospital start very early, and lunch was always served at eleven-fifteen. I think pain does that to people, they can't sleep past about three in the morning, and the hospital staff know it's best to get things going early to get the patients' minds off the long, desperate night and turned to the day's comings and goings. Any distraction from the suffering is a blessing, and as the sun rises there is a renewal of hope that maybe this will be the day when they will get better and go home, or that someone will come and visit, or that at least they won't hurt as much.

I turned my thoughts back to the rattle of the lunch cart as it stopped by my door, and thought about how I was glad I was on solid food now. But I still didn't have much appetite. Two of my favorite nurses came in the room and one said, "I bet you're happy. Aren't your flowers so pretty?"

I answered, "Well, yes, I am happy because my flowers are pretty. They smell good, too."

"Aren't you the one who's going up to LDS Hospital?" they asked.

"Yes, if I ever get up there." They gave each other a look, and they both left.

Then two nurses brought up my mail. I was still getting a lot of letters and cards. One of them said, "After lunch we'll put another hot-pack on you." I didn't need them so much, anymore, so this was a little unusual. But then she changed her mind, "Oh, no, not if you're going," and she left.

By this time, I was beginning to wonder what was going on. Could it be possible that I was being moved to another hospital? I didn't have to wonder for long, because Dr. Judge soon came in and told me that I was going up to the LDS Hospital! I uttered a short silent prayer of gratitude. Suddenly I felt so much better!

A little while later a couple of orderlies brought the stretcher. The nurses wrapped me in sheets and told me that the only thing I could take with me were my glasses that I wore for distance. How I so wanted to take my cute vases and flowers and plants that all my friends and family had sent to me. I'd counted my letters and cards, of which there were fifty. I was sorry to leave them, because they were all I had of those friends and family while I was in the hospital and couldn't see them. But I had no choice. They could be contaminated, and the hospital couldn't risk it.

They put me into the ambulance and I was on my way. The doctor said to take care of myself, and that he knew they'd take really good care of me at LDS. The ride in the ambulance was so comfortable and wonderful just because I was leaving the County Hospital. It was during the ride to the LDS Hospital that I realized that my life had taken a turn. I was in for new experiences.

CHAPTER 3

Out of Isolation

It could have been pouring rain, with crashing thunder and lightning, and it still would have been a wonderful day. However, the sky was blue, the sun was shining, and the ground and trees were covered with sparkling snow. As the orderlies rolled me into the hospital, I thought, "This is really an experience! It's nothing to this guy who is pushing me, but it's something new to me!" It was so nice to see anything new at all.

High up on the Avenues of Salt Lake City, east of the Utah State Capitol and across City Creek Canyon, was a large hospital owned by The Church of Jesus Christ of Latter-day Saints, or LDS for short. I was taken to a room with four beds. One bed was empty, waiting for me. The nurse introduced me to the other patients. There was a little girl, Hilda, who was about five. She'd been in the hospital for a month, but wasn't very bad, relatively speaking. She had polio in one of her legs but she could walk on her own.

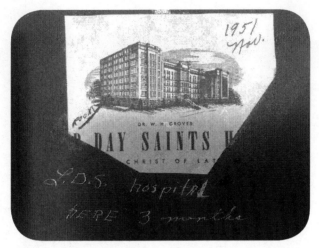

1951 nov.

L.D.S. hospital HERE 3 months

LDS Hospital

Carol, another patient, was about nineteen, and she was paralyzed all over. Carol's polio had affected her spine as well as her lungs, so she stayed all the time, day and night, in an iron lung. The only time she got to come out was when they gave her a sponge bath and changed her clothes and sheets. I thought "Oh, how awful," at the thought of having to be in the iron lung, and I was happy that at least I could move my arms and upper body. To be completely paralyzed would have been so hard.

Next to me was a little boy, Steven, who was about nine years old. He had polio like I did, from the waist down, only his back was better than mine. He could get around in a wheelchair very well, and he brought me a stack of comic books.

These were my new living arrangements and roommates. There were many good things about the hospital that made me happy right from the beginning. We learned that visiting hours were from 3 o'clock until 4 in the afternoon and from 7 until 8, every day of the week. When the orderly brought me a great big meal for dinner, with lots of good things to eat, I thought everything was just super.

That night Mother brought me my pajamas, a brush and comb, some lotion, a tube of my favorite toothpaste, and some other things she thought I'd appreciate. It seemed good to get into my own PJs, instead of into a hospital gown. After Mother and Dad left, the four of us roommates talked for a while, getting to know each other. I slept soundly that first night.

Mother and Daddy had gone back home to Spanish Fork and said they'd be back on Friday. In the meantime, my Aunt Phyllis and Aunt Erma would keep me company. But they'd only been there for a short time when a therapist, Miss Campbell, came up to get me. She put me on a stretcher, and took me downstairs in the elevator to the therapy room. Once we were there she transferred me to a stretcher that was over a big tank full of very warm water. She lowered me in with a big overhead pulley submerging my entire body except for my head.

The water was as hot as I could stand it, and it helped in the same way that hot-packs did, which was to relax the muscles and ease the pain. The tank was shaped like a figure-eight. The therapist stood in the middle where the circles of the figure eight came together and she could reach my legs and my arms. While I was still in the water, Miss Campbell exercised my legs and back, hips and arms. She would stretch my muscles out and move my joints, trying to get them back to their full range of motion. She would tell me to lift my leg or put it to the side or bend it back even if I couldn't. The purpose of this was to see how much strength I had to begin with, and then to build upon that. She was trying to help me rebuild the nerve pathways between my brain and my muscles.

When she asked me to raise my right foot up, only my big toe would come up, and my foot would turn to the right. When she would push against my foot I had enough strength that I could give her a little resistance. I could also push it down, and give her some resistance there, as well. On my right knee the hamstring on the outside could move, but not the one on the inside. I couldn't rotate my right knee. My left foot was unaffected and the hamstrings behind my left knee could flex a little. I could move my kneecap just a little on my left leg, but not enough to straighten my leg. I could move part of my stomach muscles just a little. The only other muscles that I could move were my gluteus maximus muscles. Those were the muscles that mainly pulled my leg up when I lay on my stomach.

Even though I could use my arms, Miss Campbell tested all my muscles from the waist up to see how much they'd been affected. The upper part of my body was weak, and we always worked on it, but it didn't compare with the damage done from my waist down.

Miss Campbell was a lot of fun, laughing and joking with me, and making me laugh just when she was doing something that was going to hurt a little more than usual, so that I didn't notice it as much. Therapy was a lot of work, even though Miss Campbell was doing most of it for me. I was still very stiff, and it hurt to be moved. Once I got all stretched out, though, I could keep that position.

That evening I started to tease one of the nurse's aides, Mrs. Farris, or "Ferris," as we all called her, who was feeding Carol. She laughed and gave it back as good as she got. Mrs. Hess, another aide, was helping the rest of us, and she joined in. I laughed, as did Carol, Steven, and Hilda, and I decided that I liked these nurses a lot. They were so down-to-earth, and if I had to be away from my own mother so much, then they were the next best thing. They'd both been especially trained to work with polio patients. I must say there were a lot of good nurses on that floor. Mrs. Seal was another one who was easy to laugh with. She had a knack for making the unpleasant tasks, like using the bed-pan and changing the sheets, go a little easier.

That night I had visitors from home. Our neighbors brought me some stationery. Because only two people could visit me at a time, they stayed for half an hour, and then their daughter and her husband came in. I was surely happy to see them. Right at 8 o'clock the nurse shooed them out. My dad's Uncle Clyde had also been in to see me, and had brought me a luster clay set. The next night Mother and Daddy came back, and I was so glad to see them.

My roommates and I had a lot of fun at night. We joked and talked until quite late, and it was getting so that I could sleep better. It had become apparent that Hilda was a little spoiled brat, and none of the three of us wanted her there anymore. We were busy trying to convince the nurses to move her out, when to our surprise, she was, and a girl named Marilyn was moved in. She was twelve, and paralyzed from the waist up, so she couldn't use her arms. She could hold up her head, but not very well. When using a wheelchair, the nurses would put her in the "granny" chair that had a taller backrest, so she could rest her head against it. She learned to wheel herself around by pushing the spokes with her feet, and she got pretty good at it, too. We were sure she'd be a lot easier to live with, and a lot more fun, than Hilda. How wrong we were.

I had a new doctor there at the hospital. Our physician at home had recommended that we ask for Dr. Clegg. The first night I was in the hospital he came to see me. Every day that I was there he came in, if only to say hello, and that meant a lot to me, to know that he cared enough to take the time to do that.

Daddy would go home to Spanish Fork during the week to work. Mother stayed mainly at Uncle Ralph and Aunt Phyllis's in Salt Lake because she would be close and could take the bus to visit me every afternoon. Aunt Phyllis and Uncle Ralph where so good to us throughout all of this.

My aunt Phyllis (left), uncle Ralph and their kids Linda, Julie and Kathy

Friday, Mom and Dad had great news for me. I could go up to Uncle Ralph's and Aunt Phyllis's house for Christmas! I was so happy, as up until then I'd only hoped for this. They were excited, too, and we all looked forward to it. At the County Hospital, I'd been so set on getting home for Christmas, and here I was, just about as excited to go to my relatives' home.

Wednesday, the nurses put me in a wheelchair, which enabled me to see the world right-side up again. Until then, I had mostly lay in bed. I could only be in the chair for a little while because before long I would begin to feel totally drained. It was also very painful to be lifted from my bed to the wheelchair.

The Saturday before Christmas, Steven was released from the hospital to go home for good, and Carol went home for a ten-day visit. After Mother and Daddy left that afternoon, I was suddenly very lonely. I started to cry, and I wondered what I was going to do for ten days with only Marilyn in the room with me. She kept asking me too many questions repeatedly. It was quite annoying, as most of the time I didn't know the answers, and I didn't want to think about what she wanted so desperately to talk about. She kept asking me about things such as why the doctors and nurses did this or that, or what was going to happen next. I'm afraid I got quite cross with her, and even told her to shut up once. That didn't help me feel any better, and we spent a couple of hours in hurt silence on her part, and sullen stubbornness on mine.

In the room next to mine, I had met two little baby boys with polio. Also, I had met Mrs. Curly. Initially, she was paralyzed all over, but fairly soon the strength in her arms started to come back. In fact, they eventually got strong enough to help her walk with two crutches that had a guard that went all the way around the forearm, and then another grasp for the hands to hold. She had two braces on her legs and a hip brace, too. Braces! Would that be the solution for me?

I was beginning to realize what my situation was. I knew, without being told, that I would need to have braces on both legs, with hip braces, too. But as of yet, no one had said anything to me about it. All the therapy had helped me get to the point where, lying on my stomach, I could bend my left knee to a little under a 90-degree angle. There had been minimal progress so far, so to finally be able to move a muscle on my own was cause for celebration.

As time went on, it had become apparent that I did have some muscle strength here and there below my waist. We found this out by testing and stretching each and every muscle. This made me think that my potential recovery was unlimited, and up to me. I was very determined to get back as much movement as possible. Though I didn't know it yet, the reality was that due to the damage done by the polio, there would be a point past which I just couldn't recuperate mobility.

Sunday I was allowed out of the hospital for the afternoon. Mother and Daddy came to get me and we went up to Uncle Ralph and Aunt Phyllis's. It was Daddy's first real experience with how stiff and sore I was, and seeing the pain that came from my being lifted in and out of the car really worried him. I could see that it did, but later, when I uttered an "Ow!" at the pressure, he nicely told me to "Grin and bear it!"

We had a nice visit and a lot of fun with my cousins, but all too soon it was time for me to go back to the hospital. I just hated the thought of going back. Even though LDS was a whole lot better than the County Hospital, it was nevertheless still a hospital. When we arrived, we were met by Mrs. Starr, who was almost like a private nurse to me. She was quite the character. She liked to tease. She had a good dry sort of humor, and I enjoyed her quick wit.

That night, our neighbors from home, Mark and Hilda Boyack, came up to see me again. Mark gave me some candy, and said, "I had to bring something for my sweetheart." They told me that he was our new church bishop (a lay ecclesiastical position in the LDS Church). As various visitors came to see me in the next few weeks, they told me they had expected my dad to be called as the bishop, and figured he hadn't been because of his needing to be with me so much in Salt Lake. I knew in my heart that he was just not meant to be a bishop, not because he wasn't worthy, but it just didn't seem to me that it was the right thing for him.

CHAPTER 4

I'll Be Home for Christmas

Monday, the day before Christmas, had finally come. The orderly came in to take me to physical therapy. When we arrived, Mother and Dad were there. They were going to take me to Uncle Ralph's as soon as I was done. After I finished therapy and with a rented wheelchair in the car, we were on our way to Uncle Ralph's. When we went in, the first thing I wanted to do was to play the piano. I'd started lessons when I was eight years old and had missed the piano while I was in the hospital. It was hard for me to get close enough to the piano, being in the wheelchair, and I couldn't play it for very long without getting too tired.

I was treated like an angel. My cousin Kathy was by my side every minute. During dinner, Kathy and Linda tried to get their dad to eat by candlelight, but he said he wanted to enjoy his food and needed to see it. After dinner, I called Dr. Thomason. He had told me that there was no way I'd be home for Christmas, and I wanted him to know that if I wasn't home, then at least I was at my uncle's, sitting up-right in a wheelchair.

Then Daddy and Uncle Ralph took me up the stairs, still sitting in my wheelchair. That was the last time they took me up the stairs in the chair because it was so awkward. It was a nice big home, but most homes just aren't designed to accommodate a wheelchair. After that, daddy carried me up to bed. I only weighed ninety pounds, and it was much easier.

I shared a room with my cousin Kathy who'd said to her mother, "I'd better sleep in the other bed by her. I'm a light sleeper and if she needs anything, she can just ask me." When I woke up and looked at my watch, it was seven o' clock. I wanted to wake Kathy, but I was afraid I'd wake Aunt Phyllis, too. I threw a comic book on her head and called to her in a whisper, and as I thought, Aunt Phyllis heard and came in. We were soon downstairs, opening gifts.

Daddy and Mother gave me a record player, Mark and Hilda Boyack gave me pajamas, and as a special gift I received a quilted Japanese robe that my brother Gordon, who was in Korea, had sent me. He'd purchased it while on R and R in Japan. All in all, we had a very enjoyable Christmas Day. The following day I just lay on the couch and in between playing games with Kathy, I played my record player. When it was time for me to be taken back to the hospital, tears came slowly, but not many.

Back at the hospital, Marilyn and I were the only ones in the room. Mother and I pulled the curtain around my section for privacy. This way I was not so annoyed by Marilyn trying to talk to me.

Sunday, I'd planned to go to Aunt Erma's to eat. However, a lot of polio patients were getting the flu and my nurse didn't think I should go out, but my doctor said, "I think it'll be okay for you to go out, just don't eat too much turkey." So, I went and had a good time. Upon returning to the hospital, as Daddy was helping me out of my wheelchair and into bed, Dr. Green came in and said, "You can tell she's getting better; she's meaner!" We laughed at that, and then Mother and Dad left.

Monday, Mother and Dad came up in the morning to see my therapy treatment, and then we went up to Uncle Ralph's for New Year's Eve. As the clock struck midnight, we banged on pots and pans and made as much noise as we could. To finish the celebrating, we had root beer floats.

On New Year's Day we visited with company, and then I was taken back to the hospital. I found that Hilda had been moved to Steven's bed, right next to me. I didn't like it, but oh, well. I cried until Farris came in, and then my jokes came out. She was a lot of fun. She'd tell the funniest stories, and cheer me up. She was great!

Hilda said she would be able to go home in three weeks. I thought, "Good for her, and for me, too." She was one of the children whose parents lived too far away for them to come and visit very often, and looking back, I can see why she had such a negative attitude.

On one of the afternoons that week, I was down in physio talking to Curley. I asked Miss Campbell when I could go home. She said, "Friday. Now remember, I'm not saying which Friday." I'd been in the hospital six weeks now, and I was getting awfully homesick.

The night after New Year's Day, Carol came back, and I was sure glad to see her. Rean, an elevator girl, came in and talked to us for quite a while. I would sit in the area where the elevators were and write my letters while I waited for Dad to come visit. She'd come out and talk to us. She was a Dutch girl and she dressed just darling. It was always interesting to see her, just to see her clothes. Also, one of her hands had been amputated, and she had a fake hand that looked like a glove. It didn't move or anything, it was just there, and she always had a pocket that she'd tuck it into, and she'd run the elevator with the other hand.

Once Marilyn asked me, "Will you ever get done writing?" Jeneel, an old friend, wrote to me almost every day, and fifteen to twenty pages, at that. Janet also wrote to me a lot, and the other girls. They would compete with each other to see how original they could write. Jeneel would write to me about her entire week, every little detail, "Now I'm curling my hair," and I got to know all her friends as if they were my own. Once she wrote me a long letter written on toilet paper just to be funny and different. I really appreciated the mail, and the least I could do was answer their letters.

My good friend Jeneel

Dad's Forest Service staff sent me a paint-by-numbers set, and I did a little every now and then. Dad got me a little bottle of turpentine to wash my brushes, and a little easel. I'd do one color at a time, let it dry, and then do another color. The picture was of blue birds and I still have it.

My water coloring in the hospital

On Sunday I went up to Uncle Ralph's for a little while. It was during this visit that I bent down from a sitting position and touched my nose to my knees for the first time. I'd practiced that a lot, and I could finally do it. I had an advantage in that I could work at getting better. It hurt some, and it was hard to get back up, but after practicing a little every day, I got better all the time. Being able to raise myself back up from bending over showed that I still had control of some of my stomach muscles, which is necessary to balance. But when I got to the walking phase, I quickly realized that they weren't as strong as I'd hoped they were.

I felt sorry for Carol, Marilyn, and another patient named Pat, because their upper bodies were paralyzed, they couldn't practice and exercise their muscles on their own like I could. I appreciated the strength I had, and it made me realize the blessing that I'd taken for granted up to that point of having any strength at all in my upper body. I have always felt, even to this day, that I was so fortunate to be able to do much more than I might have if I'd not had that upper body muscle strength.

Polio affected everyone differently. There was one patient, by the name of Louise, who wasn't paralyzed, but was weak all over and had a hard time sleeping because polio prevented her from being able to close her eyes.

I had many doctors and therapists. John, who was a retired German teacher from Germany, and now an orderly for physical therapy, came in every morning about eight. We would all ask him together, "What time do we go down? What therapist do we have today?"

John and his wife had come from Germany as converts to The Church of Jesus Christ of Latter-day Saints. Each day, he'd teach us a few words of German. One day he came in to get Hilda, and she threw a tantrum, yelling and screaming. The head nurse came in and told her off. That wasn't the first time she'd had to do that. Hilda once threw a tantrum because she thought that someone was going to take her wheelchair. It wasn't her last tantrum, by any means.

One day while Mrs. Sperry was working on me, she was talking about Pat, another patient. I'd heard a little about her, but I'd only seen her once. She was a beautiful girl of about sixteen. When I saw her she'd been dressed in oriental pajamas, sitting up very straight in a wheelchair. The nurse had pushed her into our room to introduce us. She had left the Saturday before Christmas to go home to Vernal, so I didn't get to see her then. She was supposed to come back the day after New Year's, but she got snowed in. She finally came back five days later, when the roads had been cleared.

Dad, Mother, and I had been spending weekends at Uncle Ralph's house, and, despite the heavy snow, we had been able to go back to the hospital every Sunday night. My Uncle Ralph's house was not far from the hospital. As I said, that winter of 1951-52 was very snowy. Every Sunday I wished that it would snow so much that we couldn't get back to the hospital. However, my dad had bought a new kind of tire—snow tires—and we went right up that road, passing cars that had slid off the road. How I wished he'd not bought those stupid tires!

In the middle of the week I received a letter from Janet. She wrote that Rex Pinegar was in town. He had been our Sunday School teacher before the Navy took him to serve in the Korean War. He was six years older than me, and I have to admit, I had a little crush on him. He was going to bring the church gang up to see me Friday afternoon. Friday morning the nurses started to dress me. Aunt Phyllis had loaned me two pairs of slacks, and

I had one, already. Mother bought me a jersey, which was really popular then. I already had two others.

At 3 o'clock Rex and my girlfriends arrived. Jane and Diane came in first, as only two people were allowed in the room at a time. They brought me some magazines. They stayed about ten minutes or a little more, and then Lois, Myrna, Louise, and Donetta came in, two by two. Last of all Janet and Rex came in. Janet was my best friend. Rex was a very religious guy, and he also had a very cute personality. When they were all ready to go, Rex wheeled me out to the waiting room to say good-bye to everyone. Then he wheeled me back into my room. Everyone there asked, "Is he your boyfriend?" I told them the truth, which was that he wasn't, but maybe I should've let them think he was. About a week later, when Rex was returning to Salt Lake to go into the Navy, he stopped in to see me. After that, we started writing to each other. His letters were all very spiritual.

By now, Dad had rented a wheelchair so I could be in it anytime I wanted, which was all day, except that when Mother came I would lie down. There was a triangle above my bed that I could grasp. I could swing on it from my bed to the wheelchair and back again so that I could get myself from one to another, if someone would lift my legs. Mother would push the triangle to me when I was in the wheelchair, I'd grab it, and swing myself to the bed, and then she'd lift my legs up onto the bed.

It was Friday night and I was waiting for Daddy to come. I was sitting out in the hall on the main floor, looking down the corridor. As the people came in, a lady would stop them right until 7 o'clock, when visiting hour began. There would always be a mob, and when she let them go it was just like a herd of cattle. There were always a lot of kids out in the hall in wheelchairs, but I was usually the only one looking for a visitor on Friday nights.

I would sit there and look down the hall, then up at the clock, then I'd go get a drink of water. If it got to be two minutes after seven, I'd be afraid Daddy couldn't make it. The snow was so bad I was always afraid that maybe he wouldn't be able to get through. But he always did. So, then I was glad for his new snow tires!

CHAPTER 5

Standing Up

Sitting there waiting that night, I thought back to the Monday before. We'd all been down to physio, as we called it. Marilyn was in her wheelchair and Carol and Pat were down with their arms in swings that hung from the top of their wheelchairs. We all watched Curly walk the parallel bars. She had braces on both legs with a hip brace attached. I started to tease Mr. Greggerson about my walking. I said, "When are you going to stand me up?" To scare me, he said, "right now." But of course, I knew that he was kidding. Then about an hour later he wheeled me over in front of the bars.

I said, "Are you g-g-going to s-s-s-stand me up?" I started to shake all over. He stood just inside the parallel bars, and wheeled me to face him. He told me to take hold of the bars, and then grasping me under the arms, he raised me up and locked my knees, pressing knee cap to knee cap. I can tell you one thing, it sure seemed good to see the world from full height again.

When I went back upstairs to my room, I was so excited that I'd stood on my own two feet that I told all the nurses that Mr. Greggerson had stood me up. They all laughed like it was the most hilarious joke, and I couldn't figure out what was so funny. Not to be left out, I kind of went along with it and laughed, too. Later it dawned on me what it actually meant, and I got the joke.

Suddenly, my reverie over, I looked down the hall, and there was Daddy! We went to my room. He had brought a box, and when I opened it up I saw that it was pajamas and a robe that my brother Gordon had sent from Japan. The pajamas were red with a dragon design, and the robe was a light blue with beautiful flowers embroidered on it. The flowers matched the pajamas. Gordon had been on the front lines in Korea for five months, and had been in Japan again for some R and R. He had called home from Japan before Christmas, but Daddy had been the only one there to talk to him.

That weekend we went up to Uncle Ralph's again. Daddy took us for a ride. We watched television and made some Rice Krispy Squares. Kathy stayed right by my side as usual. It was snowing again Sunday night, and I wanted to stay until Monday morning, but Daddy had to get back home to work.

Back in the hospital, Mrs. Hess came in one morning. She got out all my clothes, laid them across my legs, and said, "Ok, Nielson, it's time to learn to dress yourself." I was taken aback, because up to that point, someone had dressed me every morning. "Are you kidding? I can't dress myself." I don't remember that she said anything, she just walked out. I thought, "Well, this is going to be fun. Let's see what I can do." No one was in the room where they could actually see me, but both Marilyn and Carol could hear me, so I decided that I'd tell them what I was doing in a stop-action play-by-play.

I managed to get my pajamas off without much difficulty. I slid them down, bent my leg with my left arm, and then by using both arms, I pulled the pajama leg down and off my foot. Then I'd repeat for the other leg. Then I had to somehow lasso my underpants with one foot, and that took a while, and then the second leg opening was a little easier, then my bra, and then one foot and another into my slacks and then my jersey, and finally each slipper. I yelled out what I was doing as I did it, keeping Carol and Marilyn entertained. They laughed the whole time. I couldn't say how long it took, but I've dressed myself ever since, except for when both my legs were in casts, and after surgery. I decided that if I was going to learn to do anything, it was going to be a challenge at first, but if I kept at it, it would gradually become easier. I guess that's true for anyone, except that what was easy for other people, and had been for me before I got polio, was now harder.

We had many nurses in the hospital. Mrs. Starr gave me my bath. One day she suggested that we try to put me in the bathtub. She just picked me up and plunked me into the tub. That was a scary experience. It was a claw-footed tub sitting out in the middle of the room, and when she lowered me into the water, the motion of the water made me feel as if I'd tip over if I didn't hold onto the sides of the tub. I didn't have much balance. I was scared that whole first time. I wasn't used to sitting without any support against my back. But I learned that I wasn't going to go over, and the next time wasn't as bad.

After that she suggested that she weigh me. She took me in her arms and weighed us both, and then subtracted her own weight. I weighed eighty-one pounds. I was 5' 2" and had weighed 98 pounds before I'd gotten polio. I thought that was awful that I'd lost so much weight, but then I found out that Marilyn only weighed 63 pounds. She very seldom ate anything because she was a fussy eater. Once I offered to feed her, but after that I decided that the nurses were getting paid to deal with her, and I wasn't. When Marilyn's mother came to visit, sometimes she would bring food, but whatever it was, it was never good enough. I later learned that Marilyn only lived into her thirties, but she never ate anything but candy bars and Coke. Her mother could never tell her no. She eventually starved of malnutrition.

Shirley weighed just 69 pounds, and she was twenty years old. Pat, who was sixteen years old, weighed in at 63 pounds. She really did try to eat to gain some weight back, but she never did get much of it back. The nurses would bring up milkshakes for the other girls, but I didn't get hardly any because I was only a little under-weight. They couldn't weigh Carol because she was too large to be held and totally paralyzed. She was over-weight, but the rest were almost like emaciated concentration-camp survivors. I was getting very tired of the hospital food, but I still ate it so I could get stronger.

I got very attached to the other polio patients. Ila Marie, who was four years old, was very sweet. She'd smile and talk pleasantly to me, and I never heard her complain. She'd lie in her room that she shared with Pat and Shirley, and she'd have a little doll in each hand. She could bend her elbows enough to put them on her stomach, and she'd play with them like that. Her parents must have lived far away, because they weren't able to visit her very often.

The two baby boys were finally sent up to pediatrics. I missed those two babies. I'd gotten so I could hold them and take them for rides. When they would sit out in the hall, strapped into their wheelchairs, Marilyn and I would play with them.

Carol found out that she was going home on the first of February. I would certainly miss her. Her mother brought us magazines, and I'd read to Carol almost every night. The stories were sad and then happy, and we'd laugh and cry together. We'd play Chinese checkers, too, and I'd move Carol's marbles for her, as well as my own. Carol was engaged to be married, and I'd write letters for her to her fiancé, who was in Korea. Shirley had a television set, and Marilyn spent a lot time in front of it. I didn't much care for it, and besides, I had a lot of letters to answer. We used to tease her about never being in the room.

Once more it was Friday night, and again I was waiting for my dad. It was two minutes after seven, and he still wasn't there. Mother had told me earlier not to look for him, as it was awfully snowy, but then he came in, and Grandpa, who was up from Ephraim, was with him. Grandpa handed me a box of candy and then wheeled me down to the waiting room where Rue, my cousin from Ephraim, and his parents, my Aunt Erma and Uncle Jake were waiting to see me.

That weekend was Daddy's birthday. Erma had a surprise party for Dad. I sat on a regular kitchen chair for the first time since I'd gotten polio and played Canasta with Grandpa, Dad, and Rue. It meant so much just to sit on a regular kitchen chair. It signified progress on the road back to normalcy.

Later, Uncle Ralph's family came over. When dinner was ready, Stan and Daddy each held me on either side, and I walked, albeit hanging onto them good and tight, to the dining room. I had to really throw my knees back because there was no muscle there to keep them from buckling. It was quite a milestone for me.

That night before we went back to the hospital, Daddy and Uncle Ralph walked me around the living room again. After Mother and Daddy left me at the hospital that night, I lay thinking. Mother and Dad had been so wonderful while I'd been sick. I'd never realized before how great my parents were. I did realize that I was very fortunate in that I saw my parents so often, especially when I thought of Ila Marie, whose parents lived in Idaho, and who had other children at home, and so couldn't come down and see her very often. My parents and I always had lots to talk about, and they were always interested in everything that I had to say. Mother had come every single day I was in the hospital, except for two days when she'd had two teeth pulled. I don't know what I would have done without her being there.

My parents, Merrill and Doris

I've also been so grateful for my knowledge of the Gospel of Jesus Christ. I don't know how people who have problems in their lives survive if they don't believe in the Savior or know that the Spirit can be with each of us when we need it. As I look back, it seems to me that the girls who had the Gospel in their lives, or a belief in God, were the ones who were the happiest and most positive about their future. Curly wasn't a Church member, but she had a lot of faith in Heavenly Father. Pat, whose family was very strong in the Church, also had a lot of faith. Carol had no interest in religion and had lived a carefree life in her teenage years. Marilyn never talked about religion at all.

I don't think I was pre-destined to get polio, but I had faith that Heavenly Father wouldn't have allowed me this illness if there wasn't something to learn from it. My strongest feeling was that Heavenly Father knew me personally, cared about me, and that I was in His hands. Spencer W. Kimball, in his book *Faith Precedes the Miracle* talks about how the Lord lets things happen in the natural course of things, but if there is a specific reason, He will intervene from time to time. My polio was part of the natural course of mortal life and God intervened through those who showed me so much love and care.

One day, the floral shop sent me up a gift. The little box looked as if it could have held a corsage. When I opened it I found a little plaster cow. His horns were made in a circle as if they were a halo, and to it was connected a note which read: "HOLY COW! GET WELL!" I never found out who had sent me such a funny gift!

Another weekend passed. I dreaded the new week coming because Carol had gone, and there would be just Marilyn and me in the room. After Dad had put me into the hospital bed, I started to cry. It wasn't just a few sniffles, either. I really let it go. I hated to cry in front of Mother more than I did in front of Dad because Mother always took it so hard. "It does you good to cry every so often," Daddy said.

The next morning, I got up and started to paint. I had the whole morning. But after I'd painted just a little bit, I couldn't do any more until it had dried, so I took up my embroidery and went in to talk to Curly, Pat, and Louise. When the meal trays came–something I always dreaded because the food just wasn't that good–Mrs. Hess came in to feed Marilyn. She said, "I think they're going to move you kids down to Room 208." It had just two beds, and was at the end of the hall.

"Oh," I said, "Why can't we stay here?" Mrs. Hess said they weren't allowed to put surgical patients in with polio patients, and so they were wasting two beds. I thought it'd be awful to be in a room with just one other person for company, especially if it had to be Marilyn, and at the end of the hall so far from civilization!

I went down to therapy to practice walking, then came back to rest. I had just gotten into bed when Mrs. Hess came and started putting things on my bed from my closet and table and said, "We're going to move you now. I've seen to it that you'll be by the window." I did appreciate that at least I'd be able to look out the window. My new room was about half the size of the other one. It had a tiny closet which would hardly hold anything. It didn't have any space to put my things except a dresser drawer.

One day we heard a noise. I found out the funny noise was Kirk, one of the boys who was in the iron lung. He had been moved to a rocking bed that went up and down. This was to help his muscles get stronger and learn to breathe on their own. He regularly cussed and swore and yelled out vulgar phrases. The claim was that he'd get well if it wasn't for his awful disposition.

Kirk went home at one point. The hospital sent a resuscitator home with him, so he could use it when he was having a hard time breathing. He was just as grouchy and ungrateful as ever. We later learned that one day in the middle of the night he called out to his mother to bring him his resuscitator, but he'd been so rude and abusive to her for so long that his dad told her not to go to him. When they got up in the morning, he was dead.

The other boy across the hall was also in an iron lung. Over a year later, the nurse slid his bed out to give him a bath. When she pushed the bed back she forgot to plug the iron lung back in, his lungs collapsed, and he suffocated. He couldn't call out for the lack of enough strength to draw a breath.

So, there I was, across the hall from two young men who had so little to live for, and who would both ultimately die in such horrible ways.

CHAPTER 6

Hospital Adventures

I began to wonder if Daddy could somehow persuade the doctor to let me go home. It had been eight weeks. The doctor really never said anything definite other than it was just a day-to-day thing, and we'd have to wait and see what happened. At that time, the doctors and nurses didn't really know that much about polio. They couldn't say in each individual case which muscles would regain movement, and which would not due to severe nerve damage. Looking back, it was a good thing they didn't let me go home, and I've come to realize that it's a good thing we don't always get what we wish for.

Wednesday was Pat's birthday. We'd planned to have what you might call a polio wheelchair round-up. We were going to "round up" everyone who was in a wheelchair. Ha, ha. Pat's aunt had made a cake. Mother had brought some popcorn, and another of Pat's aunts brought an electric popper. I said I'd buy the drinks, but Curly insisted she'd go in with me. After supper, Curly and I went down to get the drinks. When we got back Pat's aunt and uncle were there. Her uncle started to pop the popcorn. Pat's aunt took her upstairs to ask a boy who she had a crush on if he'd come down to the party. His name was Lowell, and he'd been paralyzed from the waist down when the doctor had made a mistake while operating on him. He'd had operation after operation to heal him, but to no avail. He was still optimistic, though.

While they were gone, Curly and I noticed that Marilyn wasn't there. Just then her mother came by. We asked her where Marilyn was. She said, "Oh, she said that she isn't wanted because you didn't ask her to go get the drinks with you." So, Curly and I wheeled down to my room. We tried to tell Marilyn that we were all jokers, and she'd have to learn to take us as we were. We also said that we hadn't asked anyone specifically to the party, we'd just taken it for granted that everyone would know they were invited. "So, come and wipe your eyes and have some fun," we said, and she did.

When we got back to Pat's room her uncle had made a whole lot of popcorn. We did our best to eat it all. Pat was tired, so they put her in bed and fixed the bed so she could see everyone and everything that was going on. After the cake was cut, the drinks served, and all were eating, the nurses dropped in to have a bite of cake.

Thursday eventually passed, and Friday finally came. At 1 o'clock I went down to physio. When I came back, I decided to go to bed and rest while I waited for Mother. Then two of Mother's friends came in. They had brought me some daffodils. We all waited for Mother, but she didn't come. After we'd talked a while, they had to go. She finally came, though, and explained that she'd been shopping for a dress and had been having a hard time finding one to her liking.

This would be a different Friday night because Dad wasn't coming. Later, though, I had a visitor. Wallace Gardner came to see me. He gave me all the news from the church ward and Spanish Fork in general. I enjoyed visiting with him. Seeing him reminded me of the blessing he and Daddy had given me when I'd first gotten polio. I've always been grateful for prayer. Every night when I said my prayers, I had faith that I was in the hands of my Heavenly Father. Although I had this faith, I was as impatient as anyone would be in wanting Him to work a little faster, or at least according to my timeline.

After Mr. Gardner left, Daddy came after all. I was really surprised. Daddy said that his meeting had been called off. I told him all my news, and he told me all his, which wasn't much. He did say that he was going to call Dr. Clegg the next day to find out what the immediate future held for me. It was soon 8 o'clock and Daddy had to go. After he left, Curly asked, "Do you want to go down to physio and make a phone call?"

"Yes," I said. I wanted to talk to Mother. After Curly and I had made our calls, we went back up. Marilyn had gone down with us. It was past

8:30 and that was the time when the elevator girls quit work, so we took the automatic elevator. I pushed the button to go down, and it opened. No one was in it. I hurried and wheeled myself in, and just as I did, the door shut. I laughed myself silly, because Marilyn had to wheel her chair with her feet alone, and it would take her a long time. On my floor, the elevator door opened, and I'd just made it out before the door shut again. I was really laughing, I couldn't even talk, not even to tell the nurses what I was laughing about.

After a while the elevator came back again, and when it opened, Marilyn and Curly were in it. Farris, a nurse, rushed Marilyn and me down to our room because it was past our bedtime and we were supposed to be in bed. While she was getting me ready for bed, Farris told us a story about something that had happened when she'd just started nursing.

"There was an old lady who'd just come from the operating table," said Farris. "They told me to go in and watch her because she kept wanting to get up. So, I did, and every time she tried to get up, I'd push her down again. Then all at once she quit trying to get up. A nurse came in, looked at her, and said: 'Call the doctor. It looks like she's dead.'"

Farris continued: "The lady was dead, so they put her on a stretcher and told me to take her up to the morgue, which was on the top floor. Like a dope, I took the automatic elevator. We went up a floor and then I didn't know how to work it, so I got out and went to ask a nurse. When I returned to the elevator, it had gone up with the dead lady riding alone, and was coming back down, again. I caught it, and was finally able to get the lady up to the morgue."

"When I got there, another nurse helped me move her to one of the morgue's stretchers. When I lifted up her head to put a brick under her neck, which we did to hold the neck solid, green stuff came out of her mouth. I thought she must still be alive and was vomiting. I ran for the elevator and after I was half-way down I thought 'she couldn't come back alive after all that,' so I went back up and got the empty stretcher!"

"Oh Farris, what a character you are," I said.

"Well, I'm a pretty darn good nurse now," she laughed.

"You bet!" I said.

Saturday came with good news and bad news. The bad news was that Curly was going home, the good news was that I was going to move into

Curly's room with Pat because Shirley had gone home the week before. However, I was sad to see Curly go. I would miss her.

I'd just finished eating breakfast when Mother came in. "Daddy is trying so see Dr. Clegg," she said. I was in my wheelchair and we were getting things ready to go for the weekend when Dr. Clegg and Daddy came in. Walking over to me, Dr. Clegg said, "We'll keep you here a few weeks more, and then you can go to Provo for treatments." Provo was a city twelve miles from Spanish Fork, and a lot closer to home than the LDS Hospital. There wasn't much more said then, but when we were out in the car I broke down.

"If he would just tell me when I can go home. I am so tired of him always saying a few more weeks. If he would set a date, something for me to look forward to. When he says a few weeks, it doesn't mean anything to me. That is all he's said since I came here." I cried. Then I looked at Daddy and asked, "So, what did he say to you?'

"Well, I saw that he was in the hospital, so I had him paged. The minute he came down, he started walking down to your room so fast that I could hardly keep up with him. He told me the same thing he always told you." Then daddy asked me, "What does he say when he comes to see you?"

"Hello!" I laughed, "But he does come every day."

And indeed Dr. Clegg did. He would put his fingers on the top of my thigh, and ask me to lift my leg, but I wouldn't be able to. Then he'd touch my other leg, but there was no response there, either. Then he'd place his finger on my knee cap, or on my shin, or other various muscles. He'd check different spots each time he came, because of course there wouldn't be that much of a change. He'd check to see if any muscle at all was gaining strength. I could never tell any difference. However, there was once when he came in and felt the hamstring beneath my knee. He said, "Grip your muscle." I had no idea how to tighten that muscle. I'd send the message, but my muscle never got it. That was on Monday, but by Thursday Dr. Clegg could feel a movement when he asked me to grip my muscle. Hooray! But I tell you, I worked hard to get that. The hamstring is the muscle that draws the heel backwards and upward. I really did like Dr. Clegg, and I knew he would do everything possible to help me get well. He was a good doctor. He was noted as one of the best orthopedics in Utah.

We arrived at Uncle Ralph's house that evening, and got the same welcome we got every week. I thought, "What would we ever do without such swell relatives who lived in Salt Lake?" Daddy took us for a ride in the car almost every Saturday afternoon. We would only go as far as I was able to without getting too tired, but I always enjoyed it. After the ride, Kathy and I played Canasta. It was a card game we played with face cards, and with more than one deck. It could go on for a long time, and made you think.

Aunt Erma called and said she was giving a party, but there was one couple who weren't able to come, so she wanted Mother and Father to pitch hit. Since all the bedrooms in Uncle Ralph's house were upstairs, and I had to be carried up to be put to bed, Mom and Daddy decided they'd take me with them, put me to bed at the party, and we'd just stay the night. Since I'd have nothing to do but sit there all alone, they decided that Kathy could come, too.

We got there early before anyone else did. There was a card table set up in the kitchen where Kathy and I were to eat. The kitchen smelled simply lush. The host was having turkey and all the trimmings. We ate until we were so full that we could only lie around, groaning while our dinner digested. After a while we were able to move a little, so we played a game at the table.

Sunday at lunch I happened to mention that I loved scones, and how I craved them now. So, Erma said, "Well, I'm going down to Ephraim next weekend, but the weekend after that, you can come up and I'll make you some scones."

When Uncle Jake came home from work, we went for another ride in the car. Before I knew it, the time had come to go back to the hospital. But at least this time I had Pat and Louise in Room 204 to welcome me. To my delight, I had quite a lot of mail to read. The room itself was set up the same as Room 205, though it did have different wallpaper, and I was by the outside window this time, so it was brighter. By then I could sit up on the bed by myself, but I needed a nurse to help me lie back down. That night after the door was shut and the lights turned off, we got to talking, telling about our experiences and cracking jokes. Mrs. Hodge came in with her rough voice, trying to scare us into quieting down, but she didn't have much luck.

Monday, when Mother came, she said she'd decided to go home right after seeing me the following day and wouldn't see me for a few days. Daddy kept saying that the house needed a better cleaning than he was giving it, but we knew he was mostly lonesome. I thought, "Why be so selfish, I have Mother every day."

So, Tuesday when Mother came, she had her suitcase. It would be the first time she'd gone home since I'd left the County Hospital. Tuesday night, to help assuage that empty feeling, I went down to physio and called Aunt Erma, and then Kathy and Linda.

Because most polio patients had lost a lot of weight, everyone else got shots and pills and even ice cream and malts to help build them up. But me? I didn't get anything. Of course, I was glad that I didn't need building up. So, Wednesday night when Dr. Haynes came in I asked him for a malt. Doctors can order them, and the dietitian would make them. That night I got one, but that was all. That night, after everything was readied for sleep, we started to sing. We were supposed to be quiet and go to sleep. We surely were the characters.

Thursday morning, I had physio early. Pat was in one tank, and I was in the other, when I saw Dr. Clegg pass the door. After a while he came in and said, "I'm getting a brace for your right leg." The thought of a brace made a lump come to my throat and tears to my eyes. I'd been hoping that I wouldn't need any brace at all, because I could walk between the parallel bars, carefully and slowly without buckling, though it did take a lot of concentration. My left foot was never paralyzed, and had become quite strong, and that was the only reason I could get along without a brace for my left leg, as well. Dr. Clegg had the belief that you should brace the muscles as little as possible, and I think his attitude about that was right.

After he left the room, Pat said, "Oh, Myrna, that's wonderful! You'll only need one brace." Most kids needed a brace that encircled their waist, went down their thighs and around their knees and supported their lower legs, and then attached to their shoes. I ended up with a thigh brace that locked at the knee and then went down to attach to the shoe. I felt that I should be happy I didn't need as much of a full-body brace as the other kids needed, but somehow, I was still disappointed that I even needed a brace at all. That left foot of mine had given me the impression that eventually everything would begin to work just fine again. So, the cold hard fact of an actual brace was a shock.

Marilyn had already had her arms measured for braces. I wondered how long it would be before I would get my leg measured. Louise asked if I wanted to play a game of Chinese checkers, so I sat up in my bed, and she came over in her wheelchair, put my tray on for me, and we put the checkers board on that.

That night Pat had two teeth pulled. The dentist came in after his office hours. Marilyn sat right there and watched, but I knew that Pat would rather be alone, so Louise and I decided we'd go up to the fourth floor and ride down the hall. It had just been remodeled, and we wanted to see it. We took the automatic elevator. We wheeled down the hall, and at the end we took the other elevator down to our own floor, and then took the automatic back up to the sixth floor again. It was getting so I could run the automatic elevator myself.

Because we were polio patients, we weren't allowed to go onto the sixth floor, where the little children were. But we thought we would try, anyway. We wheeled through the doors, but a nurse asked us, "Which floor are you from?"

"Two," we replied.

"You aren't supposed to be in here," she said.

"Well, couldn't we just go through the hall?" She gave her OK, and told us not to be noisy.

"I'll go in here and look at the babies while you keep a watch out," Louise said. She went into the room where Ila Marie and the two baby boys were who used to be down in Room 204. Then she came out, and I went in. I think the children remembered me because I'd seen them quite a bit down at physical therapy.

Louise had been a student nurse for two years before she'd gotten married. She knew the hospital quite well, and wanted to go up to the X-ray room and the morgue. So, we got in the automatic elevator, but we had a terrible time getting up there.

At first the elevator went down to the first floor, and a lady got in who wanted to go to the third floor. So, we stopped at the second floor, the fourth, fifth, sixth, seventh, eighth, back to the seventh, the sixth, fifth, fourth, and the second again, and finally back down to the first floor. It just would not stop at the third floor. The lady got off in disgust and took the stairs up to the third floor; it was only then that the elevator would stop there. Oh well. I was trying my hardest.

The elevator then went up to the eighth floor just long enough so Louise could get out, but not long enough for me to get out. The elevator went down to the main floor, which was the second floor, and because it was visiting hours, people crowded in. People kept crowding in, and naturally no one was going up to the morgue, so I got pushed to the back. No one seemed to know how to run the elevator. Finally, a student nurse who knew what she was doing got in.

I was laughing so hard I could hardly catch my breath, but I only laughed harder when I thought of Louise up there waiting for me in the morgue. Finally, the elevator was empty of everyone but me, and I was able to go up to the morgue and X-ray room. Louise had been waiting patiently for me. "So, you finally got here. I saw by the floor indicator light everywhere you had to go on your way."

Louise went down a narrow hall and into a medium-sized room. There was a big aluminum table and also some cages. She wheeled over to them, but first I wanted to know what was in them. The place was so quiet. There simply wasn't anyone around. I was glad for one reason, if they'd seen me, it would have been bad business.

"What's over there?" I whispered.

"Rats," she answered.

"Is that the table where they put the dead people?" I asked as she came up to me.

"I don't know, but I think so."

I'd had enough. I wheeled back to the elevator to wait for Louise. On the way down in the elevator I asked, "Are the rats for experiments?" She told me they definitely were.

We got out of the elevator and just made it into our room when Uncle Ralph and Aunt Phyllis came in, carrying a sack. "I'll put this over here, and then we'll take you down to see the kids." Phyllis wheeled me down to see Linda and Julie. After we'd talked a while, Aunt Phyllis wheeled me back to my room. "I had some crisp carrots, but I guess they aren't crisp anymore. There are also some oranges, bananas, and apples." Aunt Phyllis knew how I loved carrots and fruit.

Lying in bed that night I thought, "I've just got to see Dr. Clegg tomorrow. He just has to come in. I want him to get that brace man here to measure my leg as soon as possible." I'd heard from other kids that it took a long time to get braces.

Right before the dinner trays came, a man came in looking for me. He said he was from Fitwell's. He was a funny looking guy. I knew instantly what he was there for, and I was thrilled. He was the brace man. You can't imagine how excited you can get over something like that. I decided I'd give him a nice sales talk so I'd get my brace sooner. "How soon will it be ready?" I asked.

"Oh, about fifteen days."

"Fifteen days? Oh my, you should be able to get it to me by seven days at least. Let's say a Valentine present. That'll give you until next Thursday."

"But we also have other braces to make," he said.

"I know, but my going home depends on this brace," I coaxed.

He looked at Marilyn and asked, "Are you in as big of a hurry as she is?"

"No, I don't care," she said. I just didn't understand her. She always complained about the hospital and wanted to go home, and yet she surely didn't fight for it. She didn't even try to move her arms.

Dr. Clegg didn't come in, so when Dr. Haynes did, I asked him if he could order the shoes for the braces. He said he would, so that worry was over. Then after supper Mrs. Webb came in with an address and said, "This is where you should go get your shoes tomorrow."

That night my parents brought a book that Mr. Nelson, my sixth-grade teacher, had given me, and valentines and letters his students had written for me. Before they left I had Daddy put me to bed, and I lay there and read the letters. I really laughed while reading them. Those kids really asked the questions. For instance, one question was, "Have you had $26,000 worth of shots yet?"

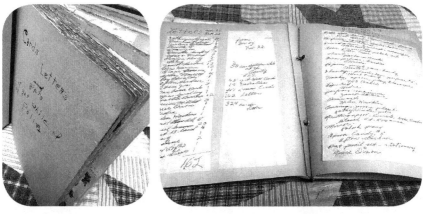

Book with letters, cards, and lists of letters, cards and gifts; 324 received

That night was going to be the last night Louise would be there, so we decided to stay awake a long time. But her husband came and brought her baby, who was just four months old, and she stayed out in the waiting room with them until long after we'd gone to sleep.

Saturday, I had physio early as usual, and then left for Uncle Ralph's house. In the afternoon, we went to the shop to get my shoes. I picked out a pair of sturdy brown oxfords which were really quite nice.

When we got back to the hospital we learned that Pat had had a hard time alone, with no one to keep her company. She'd gotten lonesome, and had choked up. Sitting there, absolutely alone, with no one around, with no one to talk to, no television to watch, no radio to listen to, and not able to do anything for herself, she'd gotten anxious. She had a hard time breathing to begin with, and lying there listening to herself breathing in and out, she must have panicked.

When she saw that we were back she said, "Oh, Myrna! I'm so glad you're back; you can't leave me alone again." I didn't know what to think of this. I couldn't imagine what it was like to be by myself and helpless. I'd never been completely alone. I only knew how awful I would feel if I were left completely alone for very long.

Mother went over and helped her adjust her pillow, and when she did, Pat said, "If only my mother could be here with me like you're here with Myrna." Pat's mother had a family to take care of, while Mother had only Dad home at the time. After Mother left, Pat said, "I simply love your mother, Myrna."

Then Marilyn said, "I like her, too, but I know she doesn't like me." She was always so negative.

"She likes you, too, Marilyn." I told her.

Mother had said that on Monday she was going to help Aunt Phyllis, so she wouldn't be coming to visit. After lunch I said, "Pat, I'm going down to physio now. You come as soon as you can."

After I'd walked in the parallel bars for quite a while and had talked to the secretary for a while, Pat still hadn't come down. So, I went up to see what was going on. As I wheeled into the room, she said, "I'm going home for two weeks!"

Right then my heart dropped and I thought, "What am I going to do with just Marilyn around?" But, instead of saying that, I asked, "How are you getting home?"

She replied, "An ambulance brought in someone from Vernal, and they're friends of mine, so they're going to take me back."

"How wonderful," I said. For her.

It was awful lonesome without Pat around. That night Marilyn and I went down to physio and phoned Mother and told her all about how Pat had left. Tuesday and Wednesday went by with me mostly living down in physio. I'd talk to kids who'd been to the hospital and had come back for treatments. The secretary would always beckon to me to come in the office and talk to her. I enjoyed talking to her and was grateful for the company.

Then the brace man came to fit my brace. It was just the outline of it. I was surprised when he answered Mr. Greggerson's question about it with, "Yes, this brace is different from other braces. This brace has only the thigh strap and the knee strap because the only reason she needs it is for her knee. I've never made one like this before, but it was like Dr. Clegg ordered." I was glad that my brace only had two straps. But I couldn't quite picture it.

I'd been getting down on the mat lately. One of therapists would help me up on my knees and help me to crawl. They would also help me do back exercises that couldn't be done in the tanks.

One day when Miss Campbell was going to help me with the back exercises, she told me to bend over from my wheelchair. She said that she would help me onto the mat. I was still terribly stiff, and I was afraid I would fall back on my heels, which I did. It hurt, but the minute I laid back down, the pain left. That was one thing that was good about this stiffness, as soon as I straightened back up, the pain went away. Mr. Greggerson came in and saw tears in my eyes, so he rushed for some tissues. He was always doing this when he thought one of us was hurt, just to tease us.

Thursday was a big day for me because it was Valentine's Day. Mrs. Jaquees, the floor secretary, said, "You have some packages in you room." Then she followed me in. Mrs. Hess also came in. They were hoping for a share of my Valentine candy. There were a number of valentines and a small package, and a large one. I opened the small one first. It was a heart-shaped candy box from Dad, and to think I didn't even send him a card. Then I opened the big package. There was a card on top which read, "To Someone Special."

"You ARE someone special, Myrna." Mrs. Hess said. That was the beginning of all the various adjectives that came my way over the years.

Starting with day one, and up to the current time, I've gotten so tired of people telling me how special, patient, brave, and wonderful I am. I didn't feel, and still don't feel, that I deserve it. Maybe it was because they looked at me with pity, or I made them feel uncomfortable because they'd not had to deal with anything like my situation before. Some of their ways of putting their sentiments raised my ire a little bit, because I wasn't patient, in fact I was impatient, and I wasn't special. They just assumed what they did about me because I'm handicapped. I got tired of that, especially when they didn't know me very well.

It seemed that so many people who knew so little about me assumed to know so much about me, and I would wonder how they thought they did. My thinking was that they'd heard I had polio, but that I could still smile. I got to a point where when Dad or Mother would start to tell me what so and so said, I'd say that I didn't want to hear it. Now, though, I have to admit that if I liked the person, or respected them, I would be a little curious about what they said.

Under the card was a big heart-shaped candy box. This was from the whole gang with all their names on it. Daddy's present had such cute wrappings, with a cupid and arrow on it, that I didn't want to open it, so I gave Mrs. H. and other nurses a piece of candy from the big box. Like they did at Pat's birthday, they would go out and tell the other nurses, so that by that night the candy was all gone but three pieces.

After they left, I got tears in my eyes to think that I was remembered by my friends. I'd just gotten into bed to rest when Mother came. I told Mother about the candy and card. Then she showed me what Kathy, Linda, and Julie had given me—a valentine and earrings. Mother had also brought chocolate hearts with our names on them for Marilyn and me.

To my delight, Aunt Erma came in. She said, "I bought you a record, but my two neighbor boys broke it, so I made you some cookies." She'd also brought a box of candy she'd found on her doorstep that was from Lila and Leo, my father's cousins. I also received two one-dollar bills and a bouquet of red and white carnations with a big red ribbon. Wow, I'd really had a Valentine's Day so far—more than when I was home. Of course, when I'd been home, I was just an ordinary kid.

While all this was going on, the nurses had moved a patient into the bed Louise had vacated when she left. After the others left, I went over to get acquainted with the new patient. To my surprise, I found out that she was a surgical patient. I guess they decided we could take surgical patients in our rooms now. We were all well, except for the effects of the polio.

At supper when Farris came to feed Marilyn, she made a crack about me, so I had to take it out on her by teasing her. We constantly teased each other back and forth.

Saturday, we went to Aunt Erma's. It had finally quit snowing, but the weather was bitterly cold. For lunch, we had what I had been craving for three months—scones! Later in the day, Aunt Erma brought out the present she'd given me at Christmas. It was Huck Towel weaving, or Swedish embroidery. Huck Towel weaving was embroidered on a piece of toweling. The weave was large enough that you could take some embroidery thread and sew it in and out of the warp and weft threads and so make designs, usually along the bottom, an inch or so from the edge. They were meant to hang in your guest bathroom and were usually for looks only. I gave one to Kathy, and we sat weaving them until supper. That night we worked on them again.

Back at the hospital, I went to talk to Ginger, the girl who ran the elevator. Marilyn came, too. When we stopped at the third floor, Lowell got on, and it was really crowded. We were almost down to the first floor when the buzzer sounded. When we got there and the door opened, there stood Mrs. Wall, one of the head nurses, and the meanest nurse in the hospital. Oh, we were in trouble, now.

Lowell had been monkeying with my chair, tipping it back onto its rear wheels, and every time he did, I'd let out a squeal. "So, this is how you do things," the head nurse said, "Always playing around." She directed this to all three of us, but what she said next was directed just at Ginger: "I've been waiting here for a long time. You should have your job taken away from you."

We all rushed of the elevator and headed for physio. "What are you going in there for?" Mrs. Wall asked.

"To work at the pulleys," I replied, because there wasn't anything else to say, and I didn't dare tell her I was going in to use the phone.

"Why, you shouldn't be in there. Wait here until I find out if it's OK." After a while she came back, and said, "You shouldn't go in there unless you have a nurse or parent with you." Then she went and buzzed for the elevator and went up to the next floor. Lowell went in to physio anyway, but I waited for Ginger to come back.

"I'm sorry, Ginger." I said.

"Think nothing of it," she replied. "She's always cussing me." I couldn't see why. Ginger was always good.

Later, up in my room, Mrs. Hodge called out, "Do you need a bath tomorrow, Marilyn?"

"It's my turn, but I don't want one," she answered. We got a bath just every other day, because we went into the tanks every day.

Mrs. Hodge answered, "That's ok with me. I have twelve patients for baths tomorrow." Then she called in from the hall, and said, "What about you, Nielson?"

"It's my turn, and I want my bath." I said.

"Ok," she laughed, "but it'll be at 6:30 in the morning."

CHAPTER 7

Home Again

It was a big day for me, because I was going to try out my brace. It was different than other people's braces. Most braces started at the thigh, were laced for about six or seven inches, and had a little strap above the knee cap and a wide strap buckled around the knee. There were either one or two straps below the knee, and sometimes around the ankle. All my brace had was a strap around the thigh about three inches wide, and one over the kneecap. There was a very simple locking mechanism to keep my knee stiff if I needed to stand. The rod of the brace went down from my knee and fitted into my special brown oxford shoe. Everyone in physio said, "What do they call this? The Nielson brace? We always knew you had to be different, Myrna."

After I tried on my brace, I went into the tank. It was a lot different than without it. I'd often wondered what a stiff leg felt like. After that, with the brace on, I walked and tried to stand alone until they made me go get my breakfast. I hurried with breakfast, put my hair up, and was back at it, again. I went down on the mat where the nurses helped me to get up on my hands and knees so I could practice crawling, and thus exercise those particular muscles. Now I was doing those exercises twice a day, instead of just in the afternoon. Later, Mr. Greggerson taught me to get up alone in the parallel bars. I practiced walking until they threw me out again, and after lunch I went right back again.

On Thursday, I tried walking with the brace and crutches. An aide came in and started me walking with the crutches. It was awfully hard, and every time I started to fall I'd grab onto the bar and let the crutches fall. I was walking like this when Mother came in. "Take your child up to bed and make her rest. She's been walking all day," Miss Campbell said to her. So, Mother and I went up to my room.

Tuesday night I was sitting out in the hall when I saw Dr. Clegg walking down the main corridor. He buzzed for the elevator and nipped in to see me while he waited for it. "Dr. Clegg, when can I go home?" I asked him for the thousandth time.

"When you walk the way I want you to," he said, and then was gone. I wondered exactly how it was that he wanted me to walk.

Wednesday I had Miss Campbell for physio, for which I was thankful. She was just the best in knowing exactly what she was doing. She was very good at telling me just what she wanted me to do and how to do it. "Now that you can walk with crutches you certainly don't want to walk in the bars, do you?" she asked.

"I don't know," I said, a little scared.

"Oh, come on now, you've graduated from them!" So, there I was, trapped! I was terribly nervous at first. If I so much as looked at something, I felt like I was going to fall. We walked into the office. There, John had my wheelchair ready for me to sit down. I stood in front of the chair and turned around so my back was to it. I handed my crutches to the nurse, and of course I had my brace on my leg and the special shoe that it fit down into. I bent my left leg and my right leg with the brace stuck straight out in front of me. Then I lowered myself into the chair. Holding onto the arm of the wheelchair, I bent over and unlocked the brace and then bent my right leg down with my hand. After I sat down I asked, "So how do I get back up by myself?"

"You rest a minute and then I'll show you," Miss Campbell said. Later she came back, locked my brace, and said, "Turn so you are almost on your stomach and then bring your right leg up, take your crutches to help you to stand straight, turn around holding onto the arms of the wheelchair as you do, then stand up and walk."

It wasn't as easy as it sounded, but I finally made it with just a few scared screams and some assistance from Miss Campbell. "Do you want to walk to your room, if we use the elevator instead of the stairs?" she asked.

"Do you think I can?"

"I think so, and you should think you can, too," she shot back. So, I did.

Later, after lunch, I was down in the office talking when Mother came in. I said, "Guess what, Mother? I walked upstairs today."

"Up the steps?" she asked.

"No, up the elevator. You ought to know I couldn't go up the steps." I was angry. I'd wanted to surprise her, and here she'd spoiled it. And besides that, she'd just automatically assumed I'd gone up the stairs, which was a feat still far beyond me, and had completely skipped over the huge accomplishment of just making it back to my room on my own power. We went up to my room and I rested a while, and then I got up and went back to physio. I wanted to show Mother how well I could walk.

The next morning, after what seemed like hours, Dr. Clegg appeared in his navy-blue suit. "Dr. Clegg, you have to watch me walk." I said.

"Ok, come on, you can walk holding onto my hands," he said.

"Oh, no, come down to physio where my crutches are," I pleaded.

"Ok. You go down and I'll be down in a minute," he replied.

"Be sure you come!" I wasn't taking any chances.

Down at physio I said to Miss Campbell, "Tell him that I do it perfect, usually. I know I won't now." Then he came in. My heart went up in my throat and stayed there so I couldn't swallow. I felt like I was going in to take a stiff exam at school. I went through every movement with my mind on each move.

When I was up and walking, Dr. Clegg said, "I don't see why we can't let her go home Saturday." I will never forget those words; they're engraved in my mind.

"Let me sit down. Do you mean this Saturday? Day after tomorrow? Oh, I can't believe it, I just can't!"

I went into the office and asked if I could use the phone. I could hardly dial because my fingers were shaking all over.

"Hello?" It was Aunt Phyllis's voice.

"Let me talk to Mamma," I said.

"What do you want?" she asked.

"OK, I'll tell you, but let me talk to Mamma."

"Hello?" it was finally Mother.

"Mother, I can go home Saturday!" I was so excited.

"That's nice." Mother said.

"I'm listening in. Do you care if I do?" It was Aunt Phyllis.

"No, of course not."

"Oh, Mother, aren't you even thrilled?" I asked.

Mother said, "Sure, I'm glad."

"Well, you don't sound like it," I said. On my way upstairs I thought, I know she's glad she can move out of Uncle Ralph's home and go back to Spanish Fork. I couldn't figure my parents out. Ever since I'd gotten polio they'd wanted me to get better soon, but every time I did something new, they didn't seem to care. But I knew they really did. Looking back now, I think that maybe my Mother wasn't ready to have my care completely turned over to her and my Dad alone. Perhaps she didn't feel confident in their ability to do the things for me that I would need them to do. Maybe she had assumed that I would be walking a lot better when I went home. I think this was the main thing for her.

Most kids would have yelled the news around the division, but I knew it would only make Marilyn feel bad. I'd heard Dr. Clegg say she could go home the following week. So, I went in and told Marilyn that she was going home. And then I told her my news. I was waiting out in the hall for Daddy when he came. I didn't say anything until we were in by my bed.

"I can go home Saturday," I exclaimed.

"Well, good," he said in a dry voice.

"Aren't you even happy?" I asked.

"Sure," he said.

Oh well, I guess Mother and Dad didn't know how to express their feelings. I knew they wanted to go home to Spanish Fork and not spend so much time in Salt Lake.

"When I get home, I can practice standing, and soon I'll be able to do the dishes, and Mother's hair, and just everything." I was really making plans, but soon Daddy had to go.

Later Mrs. Hess came in. "I've come to say good-bye, Myrna. I won't be working tomorrow or Saturday."

"Well, Mrs. Hess, I've surely enjoyed your company," I said.

"I've enjoyed yours, too, Myrna. I wish we had more patients like you."

While I was still in bed Dr. Clegg came in. Marilyn started to beg him to let her go home sooner.

"You can go home a week from now. You have to wait until we fix your brace," he told her.

"Why couldn't I come back and have it fixed?" she asked. Finally, Dr. Clegg gave in. Then he said to me, "You don't want to go home until tomorrow, do you?"

"Tomorrow! Can I go home today?"

"No, we'd better keep it tomorrow." he said.

"But Dr. Clegg, today is Washington's birthday. Dad will be here today." I begged.

"OK, then you both can go home today."

I dressed, and tried to clean up as much as possible. While I was doing this, the student nurse came in and said she was ready to wash my hair. I got on the stretcher and she took me into the sink. There I slid up on the stretcher so my head was in the sink. It wasn't much of a wash. She was too gentle to wash hair, but I liked her.

Mother and Dad came in while I was still having my hair washed, and then when I was back in my wheelchair, she blew it out with a hair-dryer. By the time I was through, Mother and Dad had everything cleared up and were ready to go. The wheelchair? No, I wasn't going to take that with me. I knew that if I did, I'd want to depend on it too much.

We went over to Uncle Ralph's for lunch, and then started home. HOME! During the ride home I thought about a lot of things. I thought of what wonderful parents I had, how they'd stuck with me all along.

Then I thought of the piano. If I started to take lessons again, that was if I could, because of my legs and my balance, would Mother and Dad be like they were before about my playing? They never forced me to play, but they gave me the feeling that if I hadn't practiced by 5 o'clock, then I must not be enjoying it anymore. Also, if I ever played just for enjoyment, maybe just two pieces, and then quit, they'd say something like, "You sure can't stay at the piano very long."

I guess that is why I would only practice my hour and that was all. But, I really, down in my heart, loved the piano. After one of my aunts down in Ephraim got a piano I used to like to play it because I could get up when I wanted to and feel free of any criticism.

"Here we are in Springville! Almost home," Daddy said. Before we knew it, we were coming around the bend, which we called "Maggie's

Bend." Then we passed the "WELCOME TO SPANISH FORK" sign, took another turn, and there I saw the Arch Theater, and after about six blocks, we turned the corner.

There it was, my home. It was the house in the middle of the block. Tears came to my eyes, and before I knew it, I was crying. It was so good to be home. While Dad got out to unlock the door I smiled at Mother and said, "I bet Gordon even cries when he comes home. It'll be a year for him."

"I bet he will, too. Isn't it funny, you cry for joy and you cry for sorrow," Mother said.

Daddy picked me up and carried me in. I sat on a kitchen chair and cried some more. After a few minutes, I decided I wanted to walk through the house. I first went into the dining room and then into the front room. I thought about how the last time I'd walked through this house it hadn't been with a brace and crutches.

Then I went into my bedroom, my favorite room. I looked around at all my things. I looked at the yellow and white ruffled curtains which Mother and I had picked out a couple years before. Then I looked at all the storybook dolls on top of my dresser. Nothing had changed, but I had.

I went back to the living room. I sat in the red chair which was by our big front window. I could see a little bit of the front yard, and across the street was Dad's white and green Forest Service office surrounded by the gravel yard where they kept their equipment. Next to it was a long white garage, and there was a lot of snow on the ground, there, too. It was such a happy moment. Everything looked good. I thought I'd soon be well, but the best thing about it was that I wasn't in the hospital anymore.

Dad's office which was across the street from our home

Just then Dad came in. Here's the list of your school classes," he said. Mr. Cornaby, our principal, had given it to him. I looked over my classes and marked the ones I wanted to take. Dad said that Mr. Cornaby would be over later.

Then I called Jeneel in Springville. She was very surprised to find that I was home, and promised to come over the next day. Then I called Janet. Afton, Janet's mother, answered and she could tell it was me. When Janet came to the phone she asked how long I would be home. I said I was home for good, but even as I said it, I could hardly believe it. It was just too good to be true.

Janet said she'd be right over. I'd written Janet on Tuesday that I might be home in three weeks, but not to tell anyone, so she was really surprised that I was home so soon. While I was waiting for Janet, I called up Lois. She didn't know who I was until I asked her if she was getting married in the spring.

"Oh yeah!' she said.

"That fortune teller we had at Halloween!" We talked for a while and then she said that Louise was having a party. She wanted me to come, but I wanted to spend my first night at home.

I'd just hung up when Janet came. She was one of the first of my friends to see me walk. I sat in the red chair, and she sat cross-legged on the floor in front of me. She reached out and touched my leg, and asked me if I could feel her touching me. I said yes, I could, and that polio doesn't affect what you can feel. Janet got me caught up on all the news.

My dear friend Janet

During this time kids kept calling me to say hello and see how I was doing. When they'd gotten to Louise's party, Lois, who had gone, too, told them I was home.

Later, in bed that night, Daddy took me through my exercises, which consisted of bending and moving my legs into every possible position. It still hurt quite badly, but I was determined to get all straightened out before I went back to physio in Salt Lake City, which was three weeks off. After I was through with my exercises Daddy surprised me when he knelt down with Mother and said, "Let's have a prayer." We'd never done that before, although we had said prayer at the meal table. After that night it became a nightly habit.

We soon started having company. All of the gang came on Saturday afternoon, except Janet, who'd gone to Provo to shop. Even Jeneel, who'd been one of my best friends until she'd moved to Springville in fifth grade, came. The all stayed for about two hours.

Carol and Hilda Boyack came after the others had left. Hilda and her husband Mark were our neighbors, and Carol was their married daughter. Her husband had been called up to duty in the Korean War so she was staying with her parents. They were wonderful neighbors, and we really became close friends. They asked, "Why didn't you let us know you were home? We just took a guess when we saw the bedroom light on." Carol and Hilda came over a lot after my return. They were a pair that I loved to visit with.

My good friend and neighbor Carol whose husband was in Korea

That day, Daddy took my good spring-filled mattress off my bed, and replaced it with an old cotton mattress. I needed a firm bed, in order to keep my spine as straight as possible. I didn't mind it though because it felt good.

The next day, Sunday, we had a lot of company, too, and by that night I was pretty tired. On Monday I got all my letters and gifts together and wrote down who gave each of them to me. I'd already sent thank-you notes in the hospital, but I wanted to keep a record.

Mr. Cornaby came to visit. He went over my tenth-grade classes with me. He asked me, "Do you want to be a nurse, Myrna?" My answer was a short "No." I'd had enough of nurses by then, and I didn't see myself doing what nurses did. He said that he'd made an announcement at school that I was home, but that maybe everyone shouldn't all come at once to see me, or I'd get too tired. Later I thought that maybe some of the kids didn't come at all because of that, and I wished that he hadn't said that. He visited for as long as he could, and before he left he said, "We'll have your home teacher, Mrs. Francom, come down one of these days."

Miss Jensen, one of my favorite teachers, had been down the day before and had brought my books. When Mrs. Francom came to visit, she told me I could go at my own speed. I had a lot to catch up on. I'd been in the hospital exactly twelve weeks, which meant that I was behind in my schoolwork that much.

One night Jeneel asked if any boys had come to see me. I said, "Yes, Paul Hair and John Davis came on Monday night." That had been awkward. They didn't know what to say, and I didn't, either. One thing I really didn't like about not being able to get up was that when they came into the kitchen where I was still sitting at the table with my mom, I couldn't take them into the living room, where at least we could attempt a conversation without the added impediment of trying to think of something to say in front of Mom.

Paul and John were boys in the neighborhood, boys that I'd grown up with, though I have to admit that maybe I still had a grade-school crush on Paul. He and I had dated in sixth grade, going to movies and such. I'd taken him to a party that fall before I'd gotten polio. He'd tried to put his arm around me at a movie, but I hadn't let him. Later Louise told me that he'd felt bad. I have to admit that I still liked him a lot, though I'd pretty much given up on him because he'd started looking at other girls. I'd also taken John to a party before I'd gotten polio. We hardly knew what to say to one another, and needless to say, they never came back to visit me again.

Helen Hawkins, my piano teacher, came with a cute cup and saucer. She said, "Whenever you're ready to take piano lessons again, I'll come down."

"Thanks a lot. I've tried to play, but it was sort of difficult to keep my balance." One night I fell to one side while playing. After that I very seldom played. I had the feeling that I wasn't in the right position to play. I felt that if I could get up and walk to the piano, it would be different.

Every day I tried to stand, but I just couldn't for very long. I'd either fall forwards or backwards. I wanted so much to stand and do things without support.

On Friday, Mrs. Francom came again. At first I thought that I wasn't going to like her, but I soon learned to love her. She came on Mondays and Fridays. I was busy all week long. I tried to figure out how much homework I'd have to do each week to finish by May.

One night in bed I started to cry. I slept with my teddy bear close by, and I had to hide my face in it so Mother and Dad wouldn't hear me. I really don't know what I cried about, but honestly and truly, at the time, I didn't think I was crying because of my polio. I think it was that I wasn't like my friends, anymore. Deep down, there was still this polio thing I had to grapple with. I felt that I was going to get well again, but here I was with the brace and the crutch, and I was still facing so much hard work to walk and lead a normal life. I couldn't just jump back in to what I'd been used to doing.

Years later, it really hit me that I'd really lost out on many normal high school experiences. When I got older, and went college, I did as much or more as the other girls did. I wasn't really thinking about boys at that time; I was thinking about the big picture. At the time, I was satisfied with how things were in my life, and it wasn't until later that I realized what I had missed out on.

My exercises came twice a day. They were basically the same as the exercises in the hospital except I wasn't in a tank of water. Mom and Dad were faithful about my exercises. They took more interest in me than I did myself. Every so often tears would come to my eyes because it hurt, but I always had them push me just a little beyond where my muscles wanted to go. I wanted to be over my soreness by the time I went back to the doctor.

Nothing special happened in the days that followed. It still snowed a lot, so I couldn't go out. I practiced standing, every day. I'd be so hot afterwards that I'd make Mother turn the furnace down, and then my feet would freeze. The circulation in my legs and feet was bad. When I'd lie down in the afternoons, Mother always put the hot-pad on my feet. I couldn't get off most of the chairs because they were too low, so Mother or Dad would have to raise me to my feet. I thought that this must've been hard on them, but they never said anything.

Two weeks after we were home, Grandpa Nielson came up from Ephraim on the bus. On Saturday, Daddy took Grandpa and me out to see Cheyenne, who was Gordon's horse. Being a Forest Ranger, Dad had a lot of U.S. government horses. Daddy had a man take care of them and ours over the winter, but the man didn't feed them enough. All this time I had to stay in the truck because it was muddy and cold outside. I have a picture of me standing by Cheyenne, holding onto a fence. I had jeans on, and I had on my brace. Grandpa was in part of the picture, too.

Pictured described above, grandpa is holding the reins

On our way back, Dad said that Tony, my favorite horse, was terribly thin and sick. I felt sorry for him. Oh, how I'd like to go pet him and take him for a ride.

Sunday, when we went to take Grandpa to the bus depot, we drove through town. It was the first I'd see of the town since November. Daddy drove to where some new homes were going up. As we came back, we passed the school. I shut my eyes, because I couldn't bear to look at a place where I was supposed to be, but wasn't. During the next week, I did my studies at home as usual.

It snowed during the week, but by Saturday it was nice and sunny, so Daddy took me out for a walk. I put my brace on, and Daddy carried me out, and set me down on the porch. Then with the brace and crutches I walked slowly but surely up and down the sidewalk.

When I got tired, Daddy put me in the car, and we went down to Rulon's to see Cheyenne again. I stood with my crutches while Daddy caught him. The sun felt so good on my face while I waited for him. As I saw the horse, I thought, "Oh, if I could only jump on his back."

I stood with one hand on the fence, and the other holding the bridle, ready for Daddy to take a picture. But I was too unsteady, and if the horse moved, I felt that I was going to fall, and I just put my arm on the horse. I'll always remember that day, because it felt like I was going to be OK, and that everything was right again.

The following Monday, Mother said, "Why don't we go out to eat Wednesday night?" I thought that very strange. My parents never liked to eat out. That same night as I was listening to the radio, the phone rang. When Mother went to answer it, she said to me, "You can turn the radio up, it isn't for you." That was also strange, because Mother usually said to turn it down so she could hear. Other things were strange, too, such as Janet talking to Mother so long about my school work. Then Tuesday night Donetta asked Mother if she could come over and play records on Wednesday night. This was unusual, to ask Mother if she could come over.

Wednesday afternoon, I wrote a letter to Gordon and told him about going out to eat, and how funny I'd look, hobbling into the restaurant with my brace and crutches. By this time, I was a little suspicious. I thought that maybe while we were out to dinner they'd be getting things ready for a surprise party.

Donetta came over at 6:30 and started to play records. A man came in to talk to Dad, but he wasn't home yet, so he sat down and talked to Mother and me while he waited. I turned the record player down. I knew now that it wasn't going to be a party.

All at once Donetta turned the record player up. I thought she was rude to turn it back up while we were talking. After the man left, the phone rang. Mother answered it, and as she was closing the door, she said, "Long distance. It's your Dad calling from Provo. He's going to be late." Then all at once, a bunch of girls rushed in. So, it was a surprise party after all. Jeneel had come over from Springville, and there were twelve other girls besides myself.

When we'd all sat up to the table, Janet's mother, Afton, came in, and my mother said, "Afton and Janet did all of this." Afton was a real jewel. She was always thinking of thoughtful things to do for other people. I was at a loss for words. Afton had brought the whole meal over in the car. We had corn, tuna casserole, salad, nut bread, cake, and ice cream.

After dinner, we played games. They were all sitting games, in deference to me. I even won a prize. I think it was the first I'd ever won in my life. Then we listened to Spanish Fork play Hurricane in the basketball tournament. We got so far ahead that we were sure we'd win, but then we lost. Spanish Fork always got to the tournament, but we never took State.

It was nice to get together with all my girlfriends again. The party lasted until nearly eleven thirty. That was pretty late for a school night. Janet was the last to go, and I thanked her again.

The next morning Daddy went to pick up his mail at the post office as usual. While he was talking to others who were there, he learned that there was going to be a funeral that day, and that Elder Harold B. Lee, an apostle, and LeGrand Richards, the General Sunday School president, and who later became an apostle, were going to be there. When he got home, Daddy asked me if I would like them to come and give me a priesthood blessing. I said, "Yes," even though my first thought was that I didn't need them to come. I felt that my faith was sufficient, but then I thought that having them come would make Mother and Dad happy.

I can still picture them walking across the street to our house. We were outside, taking our after-dinner walk as we had that week, and when they came up to us, Daddy carried me in and sat me on a chair in the front room. President Richards placed a few drops of oil on my head, which had been consecrated to the healing of the sick and afflicted, and then sealed the anointing by placing his hands on my head and saying a short prayer. After lifting his hands off my head, President Richard placed his hands on my head again, my father put his hands on as well and then Elder Lee placed his hands on top of Dad's. Then Elder Lee gave me a blessing.

His words have stayed with me throughout my life. He said, "The time will come when you will be completely healed." As he said that, it came to me that he didn't mean in this life. He also said something to the effect that Heavenly Father knew before I did that I would get polio. He told me that I would have a long fight, and that I'd need to be patient. "Keep faith in the Lord, for when you are through with this you will kneel down beside your bed with your parents and thank Him for this experience."

I was crying when he finished, and so were Mother and Dad. It was such a wonderful prayer. We thanked the men, and then Dad carried me to my bed to rest as I usually did every day. After that, every time I became discouraged I would think of Elder Lee's blessing. Years later, when Elder Lee was President of the Church, there was a particular Sunday when I was really tired. I was just starting to get the effects of Post-Polio Syndrome. As I went to sit down on the sofa, I sat down on the Church News, which came in the Sunday paper. I noticed there was a picture of President Lee on the cover, and as I looked at him, I heard his words again: I needed to be patient.

CHAPTER 8

Getting Casted

Since arriving home from the hospital, I'd really run Mother ragged. It seemed that I always wanted something. I'd tell myself that I'd see how long I could go without asking her for something, but it was useless. I really did need her help a lot. I needed her to pick up a pencil I'd dropped, or get me a book, or a tissue and numerous other things. She never said anything in complaint, but would just get me what I wanted and help me with what I needed. I didn't understand how she could be like that. All I could think was that my parents were so wonderful.

The following day was my appointment with the doctor and the therapist in Salt Lake. I wanted to be good and stretched out. I was going to show them! So, I gritted my teeth and let Mom and Dad work on me a lot.

The next day, Mr. Greggerson took me into the physical therapy room and hoisted me onto the table. He said that I was doing pretty well. I enjoyed my visit back to the hospital, but I was glad I wasn't staying.

I asked about Pat. She'd been lonesome when she'd come back, but now she'd gone home again, Mr. Greggerson told me. "You wouldn't know her," he said. "She looks really thin."

"Why? I've gained weight since I've been home." Pat hadn't been doing so well. It seems she'd lost her appetite. She was so weak, and she only had one lung working. She was a beautiful girl with a happy nature, but when everyone else left the hospital, she would have been lonely. She had to be fed, and so maybe that was demoralizing. Maybe she was depressed about her condition.

"When did she go home?" I asked.

"If she'd stayed here, we could have done more for her. If she could just eat." Mr. Greggerson said.

"Poor Pat. I'd certainly like to see her," I said.

When I was done with physical therapy, we went to Aunt Erma's to have lunch. Lila, who was a cousin to Dad, and her husband Leo, were also there. They probably knew I was coming and thought they'd stop by. After lunch was my doctor's appointment. Before we went, though, I put on a full jersey skirt. That was the first time I'd had a dress or a skirt on since I'd gotten polio.

The ride to the doctor's office was nice. It didn't take very long, but I've always loved riding through the streets of Salt Lake City. It was pretty with the bushes and the trees on both sides of the road. I was hoping, though, that we wouldn't get any more snow.

Since it was the first time that we'd been in his office, we didn't know Dr. Clegg's office was the very last one at the end of a long hall. By the time I'd walked to the door, I was really worn out. But at least I could say that I walked that day! The joke was that at the end of the hall, right next to his office, was a door that led outside to the parking lot.

We went into a small waiting room. After a short time, we were shown into a smaller room where there was a table with a thin mattress on it, a couple chairs and a few paintings on the wall. I lay down on the table as the nurse had instructed me to do.

After a while Dr. Clegg came in and asked, "Was it worth it, Myrna?"

"Was what worth it?"

"To work so hard so you could go home?"

"Yes!"

"They said they missed you down in therapy."

He checked me over and the nurse measured my legs. Then he sat down and had me sit up on the bed. My stomach muscles were bad, and they stuck out. I'd been thinking of getting a girdle, but Dr. Clegg took care of that.

"I'll call and get a corset for Myrna," he said to Daddy.

"Won't just a panty girdle do?" I asked.

"No, but this won't be a big or stiff corset," he said.

We left, and then went to the Medical Mart to get it. It took some time, and I was impatient. However, the Medical Mart didn't have a corset to fit me, and they had to take one in for me. It still didn't fit right, so they altered it yet again. The corset ended up not being very big. When the nurse said that I'd need to wear nylons with it, I knew I wouldn't like that, because I didn't wear nylons. So, I decided that I just wouldn't. The corset cost $15, which in 1952, was just outrageous to my father, and he said, "Anything you really need, especially medical stuff, is just so expensive." I still say that very same thing to this day.

When we were done at the Medical Mart, we went up to Uncle Ralph's. Kathy, Linda, and Julie were just home from school. After supper Linda and Julie went to the church to see a movie, but Kathy stayed home. My cousins tried to make us stay and sleep over, and at first I wanted to, but Kathy and I got talking about her coming home with me and then returning home on the bus Sunday. And that's what we did.

We left for home early because my friend Doris had asked me to her place for a party. She and Louise were celebrating their birthdays together. It was fun, but my corset had started to hurt, and I was miserable. When we got home I asked Mother to rub my back. The corset hurt me because my spine poked out so much. After that Kathy and I went to bed. It was good to have someone there with me.

Saturday, I did my exercises in the morning and then we all tackled trying to get my corset back on. After that there wasn't much to do, and for the first time I thought that I must bore people when all I could do was just sit. For me, though, it was wonderful, because I was finally sitting up. I was with my friends, but most of all, I was HOME.

I had already asked Janet to come over to stay while Mother and Dad went to a party. She did, and Kathy, Janet, and I had supper together. Later, we made some brownies together. I was certainly glad that Mother and Dad were going out. It would do them good. They worried about me so much and were always doing things for me.

We were playing with my Luster Clay Set when Doris came in with her boyfriend and two other boys. My corset had been hurting all day. It came up to just the middle of my ribs, and really squeezed. Mother told me that I'd be more comfortable if I'd wear nylons, and that they would keep the corset pulled down more, but I was too stubborn. "I'm not going to wear nylons. They wouldn't do any good, anyway." Back then, girls just didn't wear nylons until they were sixteen, and then only to church.

Sunday, Uncle Stan, Aunt Edna, and cousins Kenny and Nedra came by. They were on their way to Salt Lake City, and they were Kathy's ride home. Our house was what we called 'the half-way house.' When people from Ephraim would go to Salt Lake City, or the other way around, they'd stop at our house half way, and it was always just understood that they'd have lunch or dinner with us. We never phoned ahead—few people called long distance then.

That was the first time that I'd seen Nedra since I'd gotten polio. She'd been going to Snow College. We'd always been so close. Nedra and her family lived in Ephraim, and so did my dad's parents. Dad had grown up there. Nedra was the only girl in her family, and I was the only girl in mine. We were also the only girls in the extended Nielson family until our cousin Linda was born. Nedra was five years older than me, and I was three years older than Linda.

When Mom and Dad and I would go down to Ephraim, I would run into Grandpa's house, say hello to him, and then make a beeline over to Nedra's. Even though she was older, she treated me like an equal. We've really been like sisters all our lives.

My cousin Nedra, who is like a sister

Nothing very exciting happened in the following three weeks. We worked, worked, and worked some more on my legs. At night, along with my usual stretching exercises, Daddy would take a long stocking and swing my legs while I did what I could. My muscles were weak to the point that I could only move my legs in about half an inch, and out a couple, and that was with Daddy helping.

Polio does one of three things: it destroys nerve endings, of which there is no recovery, or it partially destroys the nerve, in which case it is possible to gain some strength back, or it weakens them, but you can build those nerves back up and possibly regain partial or even full strength.

In the mornings, Mother took her turn doing exercises with me. It didn't hurt as much anymore, and there were only a few tears now. Every morning I'd practice standing, but I really wasn't getting very far with it. My legs felt like pins and needles were sticking into them.

When people would come to see me they'd ask, "When will you be back to school?"

"Next year," was always the answer. One day Daddy said something about my wearing a brace the next year. I jumped to conclusions and said, "But I won't have to wear a brace next year! Do you think I will? I won't, will I?" I was very worried.

"Well, we just don't know, but I'd guess that you probably won't need to." Daddy said. He probably felt bad that he'd even brought it up.

My corset was still hurting me, so Mother bought a sponge and cut it in pieces and placed strips of sponge next to my skin where it bothered me. It didn't help though; it still hurt. One day Mother made me wear my nylons, and glory be, my corset didn't hurt anymore. Mother know best! Sometimes I felt silly in the nylons, but I soon got over it.

I had a crying spell again. I wasn't sure why. It certainly wasn't because I was bored. I couldn't have been busier. And it wasn't as Mother thought. It wasn't because I couldn't get around. It really wasn't. Mother took it so hard when I cried that I knew I'd have to control myself in front of her from then on. Besides, what was I crying for? I was lucky compared to some polio patients, and I was surrounded by the best of family and friends.

As I look back on those days I remember that the sun was so nice and that the birds had begun to chirp after the long winter. By then it was

April, and I was still so happy to be home. I told Mother this about every other day, and she fully agreed with me.

Nearly every day, I'd go out walking with Dad right after lunch. Mother was shorter than I was, so we didn't dare have her take me outside, but she walked me all over in the house. It was also hard for her to lift me to my feet, especially up off the bed and from the rocker. One day we lost our balance, and Mother had to sit me back down, but we missed the rocker, and we both fell to the floor. It didn't hurt, though, and we just laughed.

Every night I took a bath. I couldn't get in alone, and Mother had to help me. I'd sit on the toilet seat, put my legs in the tub, and then she'd help me slide in. She'd have to keep a hold on me or I'd slide around. The heat of the water helped the soreness in my muscles just as the hot baths in the hospital had.

One morning we read in the paper that the Salt Lake School District was going to get out of school for spring vacation the week before Easter, so we wrote and invited Uncle Ralph's family and Aunt Erma down for Sunday dinner. The plan was that Kathy and Linda would stay for a few days. They didn't let us know until Saturday afternoon. They would often call just as they were getting into the car to come, because they often couldn't make a decision about things like that. I happened to be by the phone when it rang. Aunt Phyllis said their cousins from California were coming to visit them. She said they would come to dinner, and bring one of the cousins, Chalene, who was a year younger than I was.

We had a railing out on our porch, and I wanted to see if I could go down the steps, so Sunday morning Dad and I tried it. It was easier than I'd expected it to be. I put one hand on the railing and one around Dad's neck. Then I'd put my leg with the brace (Daddy called the brace "Peggy") down onto the next step, and then bring the other down to meet it. Going back up was harder, though. Mother raised my left leg up on the step, and then I'd straighten my back leg so I could put my weight on it, and then swing my braced leg up.

I'd just made it up the stairs when Uncle Ralph and his family came, with Chalene. I wasn't the jealous type, but sometimes I resented Chalene just a little bit, because when she was there, she took some of the attention away from me.

Monday, Linda, Kathy, Chalene and I played games, and then they went uptown while Mrs. Francom was there, helping me with my lessons.

She said she wanted me to rest and not do any school work while my cousins were here. After she left, we read books and ate candy. If anyone could eat candy, it was Kathy and Linda! If we were in a car going any place, we couldn't go very far without one or the other of them asking their dad to stop so they could get candy. Somehow, they still maintained their girlish figures.

Tuesday wasn't much different. Chalene's brother and sister-in-law came to get her at noon, and then Linda, Kathy, and I just played games. When it was time for me to rest, we read the comic books they had brought with them.

Kathy and Linda left Wednesday at noon, and then I was back to my regular schedule. I got up in the morning and Mother helped me with my exercises. After that I practiced standing, and then I started in on my civics homework. I'd study until about 10:30, and then I'd do my exercises while I listened to the radio program, "My True Story." Some other radio programs that I listened to throughout the week were: "The Lux Theatre," which was movie scripts made for radio, sponsored by Lux soap, "Jack Benny," and "The George Burns and Gracie Allen Show." They were all comedians. I also listened to "The Great Guildersleeve," which was a humorous story, "Mr. and Mrs. North," which was a murder mystery, and "Ozzie and Harriet," which was a family situational comedy. Then there was "What's My Line?" which was a quiz show.

I'd listen to the radio until 11:15, and after that I'd do math or English. After lunch, I'd do more lessons, and then I'd usually read for the rest of the afternoon. Daddy said he didn't think it was good for my eyes to lie down and read, but I wasn't a girl to sleep in the afternoon, so I had to read. I'd worn glasses since the fifth grade, until I was in eighth grade, after which I just put them on long enough to look at the board in school, or when at the movies. There was a saying that "boys don't make passes at girls who wear glasses." I recognized that my eyes had gotten worse, but I didn't think it was due to the polio, even though the doctor and my parents thought it was.

At night, I'd listen to the radio, and that was pretty much my day. I was grateful for the friends who dropped by on their way from school, or who came over to visit in the evening. It was always nice to have someone to visit with, it helped break up the day.

The doctor said that if I would wear my corset at night as well as during the day, that it would help me more, so Wednesday night Daddy said, "Let's try wearing your corset tonight. You can take off the nylons, and just wear the corset." I wanted to do whatever it took to get well faster. I thought that if the doctor had said to wear it, then I would, gladly, but there was that nagging doubt, that if it wasn't going to help, why do it? It was frustrating.

I tried it, anyway, though tears came close to the surface. I told myself that I wasn't going to cry. The tears passed, and I didn't cry. So, every night we kept it on, and I was glad for the support. However, at some point, sooner, probably than later, I did get tired of wearing it, and so quit.

On the Saturday before Easter, Daddy and I were out walking when Daddy's assistant, Ed Horton, drove up with his wife and child. "It looks like you're doing well, Myrna. We were just on our way to the drive-in movie," his wife, Barbara, said. After they drove away I asked Dad if he'd please take me to the movies. He said that he'd leave it up to my Mother.

So that night I went to my first movie in over four months. Our drive-in theatre never had any good shows, so on the way over I was hoping against the odds that they would, this time. The first movie sounded awful, so we passed it by. The next movie didn't sound any better, but because I hadn't seen it, we went. The double feature was *Three Desperate Men* and *The Return of Frank James*. If you liked cowboys, they were fine, but I could think of shows that I liked better. That became quite the thing for us—to go to the movies. There were two drive-in theaters in the vicinity—one in Springville, and one in Provo. There was also a drive-in north of Provo, and on weekends we'd sometimes go to that one. After that, we went a couple of times a week, and I'd always hope that a good movie would be playing.

Saturday afternoon two of Mother's friends came by with gifts for me. I guess you would call them Easter gifts. There was another present waiting when we came home from the show. It was from the mother of one of Gordon's friends. It was two beautiful slips and one cute pink blouse. I can remember that blouse, exactly. It was short-sleeved with buttons down the front and sparkly threads in it.

On Easter Sunday, we went to Salt Lake. I wore a red blouse with jeans because in my case, wearing a dress just to sit around in didn't seem right.

When we got to Uncle Ralph's house, Linda had a cute sundress on, and things really seemed springy. I decided right then and there that I wanted a sundress, too.

After dinner, we went up to the State Capitol building. Daddy carried me up the hill and sat me down on the grass at the top, and Kathy and I played catch with Easter eggs. Everyone was rolling eggs down the hill. It was certainly a pretty day.

Sunday night we stayed at Aunt Erma's. Daddy was going to go home, and then come back the next night and take Mother and me to my doctor's appointment the following day. These were the days when no one had more than one car. Mother could drive around in Spanish Fork, but she never learned to drive around very well in Salt Lake City, or even Provo, for that matter.

Monday, Mother went uptown, and I stayed home, embroidered, and did civics. Ugh. It rained all day. After lunch, when Aunt Erma tried to help me up, my brace slipped, and I slid under her and fell. I didn't fall very hard, though, and there was no sign of a bruise.

Mother came back from shopping drenched! If I'd ever wanted to see a really soaked person, well, there she was. She'd been shopping for her new grandson. My brother Kent and his wife had a new baby. They lived in Portland, so we didn't see them much. Mother had found some darling rompers. I'd had her get me some material to make a skirt to go with that pink blouse. She'd gotten a baby blue cotton fabric that was woven to look a little like it had been put in a waffle iron. She'd also bought me a green sundress!

The phone rang at about 4 o'clock, and it was Kathy. She wanted me to go to the show with them, in the rain and all, but to an inside theatre. Mother finally gave her consent. She was cautious with me, because she was afraid that I'd fall. Jake carried me out to the car. It was raining cats and dogs, as the saying goes. I walked into the lobby with my crutches just fine, but when I saw the big slope going down the corridor, I knew I couldn't make it. So, we unlocked my brace, Mother took one leg, Aunt Phyllis the other, and with my arms around their necks we were on our way, except that they both started off in different directions. For a minute it was scary, but soon we got it all together. They set me back on my feet and I took my crutches and walked past the candy counter and into the theatre. I sat down in the last seat next to the aisle. I was able to walk out after the show was over.

Tuesday morning, I got up, and before getting dressed for the day, I tried on the sundress Mother had bought for me. It didn't seem right at all. My corset made it look funny on me, and oh! Everything! I cried because I had to wear my corset at all. Mother and I decided we'd take the dress back to the store.

At 10 o'clock we went to physical therapy at the hospital. Mrs. Sperry was my therapist, and I was glad. She checked my weight: 105 pounds. I couldn't get too heavy in my condition. The lighter I could stay, the easier it would be for me to move. That's always been an incentive for me to watch my weight. I'd been 5' 2" when I'd first gotten polio, four months before, and now I was another 2" taller. I'd grown, my balance was really coming along, and everything was good. I was really encouraged. On the way back, we were talking about how Mrs. Sperry had Mother and Dad look at my back to see how straight it was.

Then we drove to Dr. Clegg's office. We were soon ushered into the examination room, and the doctor came in. He looked at my legs, and he was thrilled at the improvement I'd made. He said, "Your back looks fine, but let's take an X-ray. An X-ray was taken by a very jolly technician, and then I went back to my room. Dr. Clegg came in and said there was a slight curve in my spine. He held up the X-ray so we could see it. It was slight, but it was there.

"We'll need to put her in a cast immediately." He said that after I wore the cast for a while, he'd operate to put a piece of bone in my back to hold it straight. This didn't sink in at the time. Having the cast put on was enough of a shock, right then, and I just couldn't think about anything more. He made it seem like it wasn't that big of a deal, and therefore what the future would bring was the farthest thing from my mind.

I went into a changing room and got undressed, and then the doctor and a nurse put a stocking affair over me. There'd be no more of that corset, though I'd think back and wonder why I'd made such a fuss over wearing it. There would come a time a time when I'd be happy to wear that corset instead of the cast!

We went into the cast room. I can still picture that room. It was to the side of the X-ray room, and there were a couple of examination tables in it. I was stretched between two tables, with my torso bridging the gap between them so Doctor Clegg could wrap rolls of plaster around my waist without needing to lift me or move me about. The rolls looked like gauze or toilet-paper. The nurse put the rolls in water and then handed them to the doctor and he wrapped them around me, starting at the bottom of my hips, and going to the top of my breasts.

When he finished, another X-ray was taken to see if my back had been wrapped as straight as it needed to be. The X-ray showed that there was still too much of a curvature, so the doctor used a cast saw to cut the cast halfway around. He started from my navel and went around to the middle of my back. The cast saw looked like an electric pizza cutter. Before the doctor cut the cast, the nurse put it against the palm of her hand to prove to me that it wouldn't cut me.

After the doctor cut the cast open, he took tongue depressors and broke them so that some were larger than the others. Then he pried it open and raised the cast up and pushed the depressors to hold it in place. He then stuffed dry plaster gauze into the gaps to hold the cast in place, followed by wetting some more plaster, and wrapping it around where he'd cut the cast open to close it back up. When he was through, I was exhausted from being moved around so much. I was cold, and yet I was sweating.

I'd been doing so well, and then bam! They had to go and throw that cast at me. Even now it's hard for me to think about that afternoon because of how awful I felt.

"What have I done to deserve this?" I cried.

"A cast! What have I done?" Mother cried, and even Daddy was crying like men do, with the tears silently rolling down his cheeks. I remember thinking that was the first time I'd seen my dad cry.

With the cast my dress wouldn't fit around me, and my coat wasn't long enough, so I had to wear Mother's coat. Out in the car Daddy said, "We'll lick this yet!" and I said to myself, "Yes, we will lick this yet!"

I told him, "If you can be with me when they operate, I won't mind." I thought back to when I'd received the priesthood blessing. Yes, we'd lick this yet with the help of the Lord.

I can remember so well when Mother got out of the car at Uncle Ralph's. She told Linda and Kathy when they opened the door, that I had a cast. She was upset herself, and was letting them know, in her own way, how troubled she was that I had to deal with one more thing, after all I'd been through.

Daddy carried me into the house and upstairs and laid me on the bed. We'd planned to go home that night, but now we decided to stay because I was too tired for the ride home.

I decided I'd like to sit up, as everything always looks better from an upright position. Daddy brought in a lounging chair from another bedroom, and I sat in that. While I sat there, I thought about how Dr. Clegg had said that my cast would need to be on for a year, but I thought for sure that it would only be on for several months, at the longest. After my initial crying jag, I was feeling better, or maybe it was that I was in flat-out denial. I ended up wearing a cast for thirteen months.

In my body cast, making the best of it!

I decided to go downstairs. Daddy carried me down. It felt good to be downstairs with the others. Aunt Erma and Uncle Jake were there. Aunt Phyllis had fried chicken for Kathy's birthday, and had everything else that went with it, mashed potatoes and gravy, canned vegetables, and rolls. I had some chicken, ice cream, and cake.

Daddy slept with me that night. Surprisingly, I slept well, even though about every hour I woke up and Daddy had to turn me to my other side, back and forth, all night long. When I lay down on my back, my chest and stomach flattened away from the rigid cast, so I could get a little relief from it pressing on me all the time.

The following morning, the sheets on the bed were all wet from my cast. The doctor had told me to sleep with it uncovered, so it would dry faster.

The cast hurt underneath my arms, so Daddy called the office to see if we could come down. The nurse said they could trim it a little so it'd be more comfortable. I put on my jeans, but I couldn't button them. I took a long safety pin and hooked each side of the top of the zipper to it.

We said good-bye to Aunt Phyllis, and went down to the doctor's office. A nurse trimmed the cast under my arms for me. I told her it also hurt on my left hip, but she said that she couldn't do anything about that.

From there we went straight home. When we got there, Daddy laid me down on the bed. Tears welled up in my eyes, but I told myself, "How will crying help?" so instead, I started singing.

When I got up to walk, the cast really hurt my hip. I walked into the kitchen holding on to Daddy's arms, while he walked backwards before me. When I got to the table, I was all out of breath. Mother tied a towel around me as a bib, because I couldn't bend over, and I slopped food all over. Once I got used to the cast, I did get better at not getting food all over myself.

Later we tried to see if I could walk with my crutches. It was impossible. They just didn't seem to fit under my arms because of the cast. So, from then on, I had to walk holding onto Mother or Dad's arms.

I went on with my studies as before. Friday, when Mrs. Francom came, I told her about my cast. She was really surprised, because she'd always thought that my back was so straight. To the naked eye, it was.

The day after we got home, I stayed in bed for a while. Mr. Cornaby, the school principal, came down to see me, and he didn't know about my cast until I told him. Mother cried when she saw him because she thought he had known about it and had come to see me because of it. She'd thought he'd come to offer sympathy, but when she found out he hadn't even known about it, brought it all back fresh into her mind again, and so she cried again.

Sunday, Rex came in to see me after Sunday School. He caught me when I was still in bed. He said that he was going to bring the girls in my Sunday School class by after church that night, if that was okay with me. That evening I wore a blouse that just fit over my cast. I was worried about my jeans zipper showing because I couldn't zip it up and had to use the safety pin again, but they didn't seem to notice. We had refreshments, and Rex talked about experiences he'd had. He always held everyone's attention. He was so spiritual and interesting. I don't remember exactly what he talked about on that occasion, but he probably said something about how well I was handling things. It always bothered me when people remarked on that. I never did like the attention.

I was hot, even though no one else was, so I unbuttoned my blouse. I didn't need to worry about being immodest because whatever I wore I always had my white cast on underneath it, covering everything up to just beneath my arms.

The next morning, I woke up sick. I had a cold, my glands were swollen, and I had an ear ache. The nurse had mentioned that I'd probably get sick each time my cast was changed, and I did. Mother called Mrs. Francom and told her not to come. Later, Mrs. Francom sent over some sweet peas. They were a popular flower to send at that time, though I'm not sure why. Maybe they stayed fresh longer than other flowers. You don't really see them much anymore.

A florist in town sent me some daffodils. That's one thing about a small town, we weren't just another customer to the owners of that florist shop. They knew us, and we knew them. I had Mother put both flower arrangements in my room where I could see them.

When Daddy came home, Mother went up town to see about some pants with elastic bands so I'd have something to wear that would fit around the cast. She couldn't find any, so I thought that I'd make some when I was feeling better.

I had to get up to do my civics homework. I'd planned to do so much each day, and I didn't want to get too far behind if I wanted to finish school with my classmates. I did get up, but I sure felt awful the whole time I was doing it.

Wednesday, I was able to get out of bed, and Mrs. Francom came on Friday. Grandpa came to visit that day, also. It was fun to have him here. He napped in the big chair while Mrs. Francom gave me my lessons. The cold had left, but I still had an awful cough. I could hardly read my lesson to Mrs. Francom without coughing. That was the first time I had been sick with a cold or flu since I had gotten polio. I was discouraged, what with the horrible cast and a horrible cold, it was hard to stay positive.

The next week, for the first time since I'd gotten polio, we made cookies. I sat by the table and mixed everything into the electric beater while mother handed ingredients to me. When Mrs. Francom came on Friday, we gave her some cookies with a drink of soda pop, and she said that the cookies were 'right good'.

Carol, my neighbor, came over one evening and cut out some pedal-pushers for me to make, and I sewed them up the next day. I'd hoped I would be able to work the treadle sewing-machine, and I could! It was because nothing in my left foot had been affected by polio.

The weather was really nice and I often sat outside on the porch. I either read or held the hose and watered the lawn while I sat there, enjoying the sunshine. I love the whole feeling of spring. I loved to be able to sit out at night on the porch and it still be light. I longed to help Daddy in the garden. Before, I'd always helped him in some way or another.

One Saturday, a couple months or so later, Mother received a call from Dr. Clegg's office to schedule my back surgery. Apparently, the cast had worked so well at straightening my back that I was ready to have the operation. I overheard Mother on the phone and could tell by her voice that it wasn't just somebody calling to gossip.

"That was Dr. Clegg's nurse. They want you in Salt Lake this coming Thursday to prepare you for the operation on your back next Saturday." I put my arms behind me because they had started to shake. Ever since I got polio, whenever something's going to happen to me that's a shock in any way, I would shake like that. Maybe it's because of nerve damage, or that my body has had so much shock to it that anything more is just overload.

I was quite busy the next few days finishing my school work for the year. I also told everyone to bring me funny books, because I thought it would be too hard to concentrate on anything else, and also for everyone to write. When I left on Thursday, I had a really great, big sack full of funny books.

We drove to Salt Lake. That night Uncle Ralph and family invited us and Aunt Erma and Uncle Jake to have dinner at the Ambassador Club of which Ralph was a member. We went into a big room which was beautiful and had a delicious smorgasbord with more food than I could ever put down. Afterwards, we went up to Ralph's and Julie put a back scratcher down my cast and really scratched it good because I knew it would be a long time before I could do that again.

When we arrived at the hospital many of the staff were excited to see me and even made arrangements for me to have a bed by the window in the exact same room I was in when I left the hospital. I saw my old hospital roommates Marilyn and Pat. Marilyn's body had really straightened out, which was good news, yet Pat looked the same as she had the last time and was still terribly thin.

Saturday was my operation. The first thing I noticed after waking up was the pain. Severe pain in my back. I really cried hard and a nurse came in with a shot and from then on, I slept waking up now and then throughout the day. Later that night my mother told me that the bone that was inserted into my back to make it straight had been taken from a bone bank.

"I never knew they had such a thing," I said.

"Yes, the doctor said that a lady was in here yesterday for a heart operation and they needed to take a good rib out to get to her heart. That rib is now in your back," Mother responded. Dr. Clegg said they had operated on vertebrae 9-10-11 and 1-2-3. After the surgery, they put me in a body cast again.

The pain and fever that followed back surgery was like none I have ever experienced in my life. Off and on through the first night I had a shot and pills to help relieve the pain but it didn't seem to help. I know that it will be a night I will never forget throughout my life.

I had received two letters, one from Janet and one from Jeneel and a visit from Aunt Phyllis and Uncle Ralph. After they left, Phyllis told Mother that it was the first time in visiting me that she didn't see me smile. Mother spent most of each day that week with me, which was so comforting. She also helped feed me as it was very difficult lying flat with the cast.

That next week I suffered from tremendous pain, fever, lack of appetite and gas that bloated my stomach so much that it rubbed against the cast. By the end of the week things began to improve. Once the pain was gone, I got thinking how awful it would be if I were to need another operation.

CHAPTER 9

The Joy of Family

While in the hospital we learned that my brother Gordon was coming home from Korea! Aunt Erma had received her letter from Gordon before we did so she ended up telling us. She hardly got the words out before we exploded with joy, we were so thrilled. Gordon didn't know about my operation because I had written the letter the day before he would have left Korea, so it wouldn't have reached him in time.

Dad arrived on Friday and had brought some fresh strawberries for me. Hmmm good! He also was excited to tell us the news of Gordon coming home but we already knew. Gordon shouldn't have written and told everyone!

I was finally able to leave the hospital the following Monday but would have to stay in Salt Lake at Aunt Erma's for two weeks, after which Dr. Clegg would check my back and allow me to return to Spanish Fork. Before I left, I had all the doctors, nurses and anyone else I knew sign my cast. So now it was really loaded.

While at Erma's I lay flat, listening to the radio, reading, and finally having an appetite because of her good food. The following Sunday the doorbell rang and it was my gang of about 7 friends from Spanish Fork, brought by Janet Gardner's father. They gave me gifts and cards and we really got in on the gossip! It was really swell seeing them again and extra swell knowing that I had friends like the Gardner's.

My wonderful Aunt Erma

At the end of the two weeks, Dr. Clegg released me but said I would need to remain flat at home for another two weeks. It was great to be home. Every day was the same routine. Mother would bath me, I would listen to the radio or read, and also got bored. I simply would have been lost without Carol's and her parents' frequent visits.

On Sunday of the following week, I lay flat on my bed when I heard the door open, and from the sound of Mother's yell, I could tell Gordon had come home.

"Gordon!" I yelled. As soon as he could, he came into my room, kissed me and said, "I thought you would be up and running about when I got home." Then Daddy came in from town and the excitement and tears started all over again.

During dinner, we told Gordon all about me. Everything. After dinner, he brought in some wrapped packages. They were gifts from Japan – mother of pearl, shoes, a fan, a fishing outfit for Dad, and other things. He shared stories with us too.

My brother Gordon was finally home!

Gordon spent the entire next day working on his Korean picture album, and I helped him. It was a tender, emotional time, having Gordon back with us again. We were all so happy to have him home, and relieved that he was there, safe and sound.

He quickly got a job at a tomato cannery and would come home each day covered with red pulp. Meanwhile, I spent the days writing in my journal, reading, listening to the radio, and embroidering. The time began to pass surprisingly fast.

Gordon began to play the piano again as he always had, by ear. Listening to him made me want to try to play too. I rolled my wheelchair up close to the piano and was able to play pretty well, though I couldn't operate the pedal.

Suddenly, it was the day before the twenty-fourth of July, the annual celebration of when the Mormon pioneers first came to Utah. Jeneel came over and took me to the children's parade that night, wheeling me in my chair up to Main Street. The next day, Daddy took me up to the big parade. It was a sultry day. We got to the corner, but Hilda came and told me to get in their car because it'd be nicer, and it was in the shade. So, Carol, Hilda and I watched the parade from inside the car.

Saturday, we started in on my walking. It was like learning to walk all over again, like at the hospital. Because of the surgery on my back, I'd been lying flat for four weeks, and after that, all I could do was sit up in the wheelchair, not walking at all. My feet barely fit into my oxfords, they were so swollen from the heat, and from lack of use which would have kept the circulation going.

Every day I practiced walking, holding on to Daddy's arms. Mother couldn't support me well enough, and Gordon was out working during the week. So, I could only walk at night or early in the morning, before Daddy left to work in the canyon.

The next day, Mother and I were halfway through our lunch when we heard someone running up onto the porch. It was Aunt Blanche, and then my cousin, Roxana, who turned eleven while they were visiting us. Uncle Ed had stopped at the corner to fill up the car, and they hadn't been able to wait. Uncle Ed, Aunt Blanche and Roxana were from Seattle, so we didn't get to see them that often. We were expecting them, but we didn't know exactly when they'd arrive. We talked all afternoon, catching up on everything, and ate and ate. Roxana and I stayed up late, talking and talking about anything and everything.

My aunt Blanche and cousin Roxana

That Saturday, Aunt Blanche and I decided that she needed some bangs, so I cut them for her. By the time I got them even, they were quite short, one might even say too short. We tried to hide them by brushing them back into her hair, but they were still noticeable. Oh well, they'd grow, wouldn't they?

My brother Gordon had been a pilot ever since he'd been seventeen, but it seemed that I'd never gotten around to going up in a plane with him, though I was always game. Gordon wanted to join the Spanish Fork

Flying Club and learn to fly. Daddy always said that he could, and that he'd pay for it, though Gordon says to this day that Daddy said he could, if he, Gordon, could pay for it. Aunt Blanche was determined to go on a plane ride, so Saturday morning Mom and Dad stayed home, and the rest of us drove over to the airport.

Gordon took Roxana and me up first. The seatbelt hardly fit over my cast, and we just took a little, smooth ride over town, but it was fun. It was the first time I'd been up in a plane; from the sky, everything below looked so little.

Sunday afternoon was like most other Sunday afternoons, quiet. Everyone took a nap. Roxana and I lay on my bed and talked. I decided to try and get onto the floor. I had a flat, hard mattress on a box spring, so it was lower than normal, and getting down wasn't so hard, but then I wanted to get myself to the front room. I told Roxana to be quiet, so I could surprise Mother, who was alone in the front room, reading.

I tried crawling, but I couldn't even get up onto my knees, so I sat up, supporting myself with my arms and tried to slide, but my arms got tired quickly. I'd rest against the dresser or lean on Roxana, who was laughing so hard that she could hardly stand up. I got to laughing so hard that I couldn't move at all. All that effort, and I hadn't even gone a foot. By the time I'd made it out of my room and into the hallway, I was pooped. After I rested, I figured out an easier way to slide the rest of the way into the front room. I sat up and put my hands behind me and pushed myself forward with my arms.

We had a lot of home movies that Aunt Blanche and Roxana wanted to see. They really got quite a kick out of them. Some of it was just regular home movies, but other times we'd clowned around, like people do when they see those bright lights and the camera pointed their way. We had a good time laughing.

On Monday morning, Mother, Daddy and I got up early for my appointment to have my cast changed. When we got to LDS Hospital at 9 o'clock, we discovered that Pat was there. However, when we went to her room, she'd gone to have X-rays taken.

One of the interns recognized me. I was surprised that he was still an intern, as he looked so old, though maybe he wasn't as old as he looked. He was the only single intern I knew, and he was ugly and thirty-five. When you're fourteen, everyone over twenty looks old to you.

We went up to surgery, which was on the eighth floor. There we waited until the nurse finally took me into the room. There was a table that could be pulled apart from beneath me so the doctor could wrap the cast material around my body. There was also a rope with a metal triangle attached to the end, hanging from the ceiling. I remembered the cobbled-together tables and contraption at the doctor's office, and was surprised to see the real thing here. I had a lot of names on my cast, and the nurses teased me about it. I was proud of them all, and I wanted to keep the front of the cast. The nurse helped me get undressed and onto a stretcher, and put a sheet over me.

Dr. Clegg came in, wearing a white plastic outfit. He sawed the cast off, and then he put my brace on and helped me to stand. I can still feel that vibration of the saw as he cut it off. I held onto the metal triangle, in order to straighten me and stretch me out as much as possible, and two young orderlies helped me to balance. Dr. Clegg put on five rolls of plaster. We had a jolly time with the orderlies keeping me laughing the whole time.

The nurse wheeled me out with the autographed souvenir half of the cast balancing in my lap. I was thrilled to be wheeled through the halls of the surgical department. Mother's first question was, "Did they hurt you?"

Later, we returned to the hospital for an X-ray and they announced that it needed to be wedged. The nurse made a wedge, but as she was putting it in, it looked different, and wrong somehow. Then they took another X-ray, and discovered that it was wrong. I knew it. "This is only the second one I've had to pull off!" the nurse said as she ripped the plaster, which had looked so nice. By this time, I was really pooped.

The following day, I lay out in the sun to try to dry my cast faster. I didn't want to catch a cold again. I found that I could stand on my own for only a few seconds, bent over to keep my balance, but it was an improvement over the time before. Mother and I were now able to walk together, like I had before the surgery, with me grabbing onto her out-stretched arms and her walking backwards in front of me.

Wednesday was both Mother's and Roxana's birthdays. Aunt Blanche made a cake, and that night we all celebrated with ice cream and cake. The next morning Aunt Blanche, Uncle Ed and Roxana went home, and I missed them immediately. I'd never been so bored in all my life after Roxana left.

One afternoon, Farris came by. It was certainly good to see her again. She told me all the news from the hospital. One of the boys who had been in the iron lung had died. I'd half-expected that he would, but still, it was sad. Farris said she'd write, but I never heard from her again.

That Saturday night we went to the drive-in. When we got home, as we went in the house, I said that it sounded like water was running down in the basement. I was right. The soft water tank had come unscrewed, and it had emptied out all over the basement! Everything on the floor in Gordon's room was ruined. I sat upstairs playing solitaire while Mother and Dad cleaned up downstairs. I felt bad that I couldn't help them, and wished that I could get up and work! It was frustrating to me that I couldn't get up and give them a hand.

Daddy had three forest ranger stations, but the one at Strawberry Reservoir was the biggest and the nicest. Our family went up and stayed there several times a year. We were often joined by family and friends, and had family reunions there.

The cabin had a good-sized kitchen with a pantry, a bedroom with a regular-size bed and a cot, and a room we called the office because there was a large table with drawers in it. Sometimes Dad would sit there and do paperwork. There were also two cots in the office. There was an old-fashioned two-piece telephone on the wall. I don't remember Dad using it.

The kitchen only had cold running water, but it was the best tasting water I've ever had. There was a metal cup by the tap that everyone drank from. The kitchen also had a coal stove. We didn't have electricity, so we had propane lanterns. It was so fun to sit around at night with them lit.

The cabin also had a screened-in porch on both sides. One side was partitioned into two rooms, and there was a bed in there, too. We could sleep a lot of people there, with children on the floor.

To the right of the cabin, about 60 feet away, was the outhouse—a very important component of the cabin. Daddy put two signs on the outhouse: Men and Women. Dad made a funny home movie there once. He had four or so of us go into the outhouse, and then he'd film us coming out, one at a time. He did that about four times, so there were sixteen people coming out, one after another. That was one of the movies that Aunt Blanche, Ed and Roxana were laughing so hard about.

At the cabin, I liked to get up in the morning, sit at the table, and look out across the pasture and out onto the lake. There was always a mist of fog above the water that would burn off by 10 o'clock. The sky was always so beautiful.

Before we'd left, the school nurse had come to see me, and had brought me a cane. I tried walking with it while holding onto Daddy's arm, but it didn't work very well. I also practiced walking with both of Daddy's arms supporting me, the way I had done with Mother.

Whenever Daddy was home, I'd walk with his support, and without my brace. Then one night Daddy said that he thought that Mother should learn to help me without my brace, too. "No, not yet," I said, "Mother couldn't lift me to my feet," referring to before my operation.

The next day Daddy had left me in the kitchen without my brace on, and had gone to work. Mother said, "Oh, I hate to put your brace on just to walk in to the front room."

"Why not try to walk without it, like Daddy said?" I suggested. So, we tried it, and it was easy!

"This goes to show how much I've improved," I said. "I have enough push in my legs to help you when you stand me up. I couldn't do it if my legs were still like they were last time we tried, in May." To my delight, I had improved a lot! After that, I only wore my brace when I went down the steps and outside.

Sunday morning as I woke, I heard Mother talking to someone on the phone. It sounded like my Sunday School was coming over for class time in about forty-five minutes. I dashed out of bed. I suppose 'dash' is a relative term, when I had to first push myself up with both arms, lift one leg out over the side of the bed and then the other, and then stand up, all the while being encased in my cast like a turtle in its shell. I put on my underwear and then put on a duster, which was a cotton robe that came to just below the knee. I had just made one a few days before. It was the first one that I'd ever made. I didn't even have the snaps on it yet, so I had to pin it.

As Mother and I were walking down the hall, my knees buckled because I was hurrying too fast. I went right down on the floor. Mother brought me a chair, and after a few minutes I was settled and calmed down.

Soon they were there. It seemed good to be part of class again, but it wasn't the same. The church ward (congregation) had been divided into two since I'd last been there, so some of the people were gone. The class brought me two books, and I enjoyed both books very much, but mostly the second one, *I See Adventure Calling*.

After my classmates went back to church, we left for Ephraim. Ephraim was such an important part of my childhood. It was even smaller than

Spanish Fork. Mother and Dad would stay with Grandpa and I'd stay with Nedra. It was easy for me to get into Nedra's house, because there weren't any stairs and Nedra took care of me just fine.

My father was born in Ephraim. His mother had died of a stroke when she was seventy-one and I was eight, but my grandpa was still alive. My father had two brothers who lived in Ephraim and who had reared their families there. There were Uncle Stan and his wife Aunt Edna, their kids Reed, Bennett, Nedra, Rue, Chuck, and Ken. Uncle Lawrence was the youngest; he was married to VaLene, and their kids were Jerry, Russell and SuZanne.

Uncle Stan had a farm outside of town with a two-room house on it. He had turkeys and sheep and one or two horses. It was fun to go out and play in the barn, and to eat the peas in the garden fresh from their pods. It was fun to take a soda-pop bottle with a baby-bottle nipple on it and feed milk to the lambs that had either been orphaned or weren't getting enough milk from their mothers.

The next day, Gordon flew down. Since it was a holiday, the airport was closed, so he had to buzz the plane above Grandpa's house so Daddy would know he was landing and go get him. I saw him first, and called to Daddy that we wanted to ride with him to go get Gordon. It ended up that SuZanne, Rue, Chuck, Nedra, Edna, Kenny, Grandpa, Daddy and I all squeezed into the same car.

When we got to the airport, Gordon took each of us up in the plane, one at a time, because it was just a two-seater. Grandpa didn't go up because he said he was plum satisfied with staying in the car, and besides, he'd liked to keep his feet on the ground.

I was the last one, and Gordon finished our ride up with a tail-spin, which was a thrill. It was only after we'd all had a ride that Gordon told us that he had to have the plane back by 3 o'clock. We learned later that his tank was almost empty. Gordon was like that; he'd fly back on fumes rather than say that he was running low on fuel and couldn't give someone a ride. This gave us very little time, just over an hour, to eat and see the folks.

CHAPTER 10

The Second Year

Towards the end of summer, friends were all going back to school. Suddenly, I found myself at loose ends. It was a boring, restless week. However, things picked up rather quickly. As it was getting closer to the time when school would start, Mother, Dad and I started talking about what I was going to do about going to high school, and how I was going to get the necessary schooling. The high school had steps to the front door and stairs to each of its three levels. There were no elevators or ramps, and I wasn't strong enough to walk very far.

The principal of the high school was Angus Christensen, and he and his wife just happened to be good friends with Mother and Dad. One day before school started, Dad went to the high school and talked to Mr. Christensen to see what could be done. A few days after school started Mr. Christensen came to the house and explained to me what the teachers were going to do to help me. I was very happy, and so were my parents.

Mother would go out and pick up Miss Wilkinson, who taught English, and bring her to our house, because she didn't have a car. Miss Wilkinson was the daughter of Ernest Wilkinson, who was the president of Brigham Young University at that time. Mr. Stone was my algebra teacher. He came down to the house once or twice a week. I'd send my assignments back to him with my friends. Ernest Knudsen taught American History. He came to the house once and brought me the book. I'd answer the questions at the end of each chapter and send them back to school with Janet.

I got credit for physical education because of the exercises I did. When I got my report card, I gave myself a grade. I always got an A. I also took Seminary with Mr. Whitehead, which was released time from regular school to study the doctrines and the history of The Church of Jesus Christ of Latter-day Saints.

B. Davis Evans, the drama teacher, came to the house, and he left me one typed page of a dramatic story about a girl sitting on a park bench. Everyone who took that class from him was given the assignment to memorize it, and the next time he came, I was to act it out. True to his word, he came back again a couple of weeks later. I performed what I had memorized of the skit for him. I knew I hadn't done very well, and evidently, he agreed, because I never saw him again. That shows what a promising actress I was.

Keith Anderson, the typing teacher, came and brought the typing book. That was about all I needed, at least until I'd gotten the basic skills down. I just practiced, practiced, and practiced. Daddy brought me a manual typewriter from his office, and I typed on that.

The typewriter Dad borrowed was not electric, like the newer models. It was a big black and silver piece of machinery that looked like a muscle-bound cousin to the telephone, on steroids. As you typed each letter, the roller would move along, from left to right, until you came to the right-hand margin, and then you had to press the return lever to take the roller down one line and back to the left margin.

Paper was always jamming up in it, and you had to be careful to get it in straight on the roller, or your print would slant on the page. Sometimes I'd be typing along, getting into the flow of my thoughts, and two or three keys would cross one another and jam up. I'd have to stop and pull them back off each other, getting my fingers smudged from the inked ribbon. The ribbon would gradually wear out, growing lighter and lighter until it needed to be replaced. If I made a mistake, which of course I often did, I had to try to erase it. There was always a smudge left. Then I went back and typed in the correct letter over the smudge.

Thursday night, as I was practicing walking with Daddy around the house, the phone rang. "Let me answer it." I said. To my great surprise, it was my sister-in-law, Bernice, calling from Portland. She said that she and my brother Kent and the two kids were going to start for Utah early the next morning to visit us. I was thrilled and terribly excited.

The next afternoon, they arrived. There were the usual hugs and kisses, and then I held Kurt, and kissed Melinda. They were as cute as two kids could be. Kurt was always smiling, and I noticed, during the next few days of their visit, that he never cried. Melinda did every cute and comical thing you could imagine. She stayed with me, in my room.

Holding my niece Melinda and nephew Kurt

The next Tuesday, September 23rd, was my fifteenth birthday. Daddy was going to be in the canyon until the next day, so we decided to wait until he got home to celebrate. Mother gave Bernice a permanent, and then we went to Heber, where Kent and Gordon had been born. We visited people they knew, and Lydia, Mother's aunt. She lived in the neighboring town of Midway.

When we got home, Janet's mother, Afton, brought over a birthday cake, and several friends brought gifts. I received a ring from Gordon. When I opened it, I knew he'd paid too much for it for me to wear it all the time, but Mother and Bernice reminded me that they wore their wedding rings all the time, so I put it on and hardly ever took it off. Melinda, my little niece, chose that day to cut off the top of her hair. She looked just like a bulldog. It was funny.

Sunday, we went to Ephraim. Everyone fell all over Kurt and Melinda. We had lots of fun. Tuesday, for the first time, I had an appointment with a therapist in Provo. He told Daddy about a new exercise which he could do with me. I had explained to Melinda that my legs were sick, and when we got home from the therapist, she asked me if my legs were better now. "Almost," I told her, and gave her a hug. The following morning, bright and early, Kent and Bernice and the kids left. I missed them so much for the first few days, but I was soon deep in school work.

I'd started practicing the piano again. One day, while I was playing, I suddenly knew that I wanted to play more—that playing the piano was something that I loved to do. It seemed to rest me, to refresh me. I had mother call Helen, and she came down and started to give me lessons. I'd figured a way that I could pedal. Our piano had three pedals, and the left two were hard to press down because they were only seldom used. So, I put my heel and instep on those two, and I was able to press down with the ball of my foot on the right-hand pedal. I had to practice at it, though, to get my foot up onto those two left pedals.

Then I started having trouble with my cast. It seemed to burn under my arms and on one of my breasts. I couldn't practice for long, or do anything where I had to sit straight up. I'd lie down on the floor to get relief. The cast would pop up from my body and not rub anymore. It didn't get any better, so we made an appointment with the doctor. The cast would need to be changed.

When Dr. Clegg came in and examined me, he decided to just fix the cast, but not change it. He made a small wedge, which lifted my shoulder a little, and it felt better. Then we went down to his office for an X-ray. My back was straighter than it had ever been.

I soon started doing my new exercises. Daddy had made the apparatus that Dr. Clegg requested, and we took it over to the therapist. He said that it was just the thing. Dad used pipes, an inch and a half in diameter, one for each corner. There were four legs about six feet high with pipes connecting them, top and bottom. The sides were five feet long, and the ends were four feet wide. Dad put pulleys on it. The lines from the pulleys went up and over the top pipe and came down, where I hooked it to my leg.

Dad took a tuna fish can, a vegetable can, and an oil can and filled them with cement. I used these as weights. I started with the lightest can, and I could change the weights on the pulleys as I got stronger. When I got to where I was using the oil can I could barely lift it, at first. Some of my muscles gradually got stronger and I could eventually lift the weight higher as I progressed, but other muscles never got strong enough. This was long before you could easily buy exercise weights in stores.

Dad had an extra counter that he used to count sheep and cattle, and I'd use that to keep track, holding it in the palm of my hand and clicking it each time I pulled the weight. That way I could listen to "My True Story" on the radio, or listen to music. I'd lie on the floor, first on one side, and then the other, and try to bend my heel back, drawing the pulley with the weight attached. I started out slowly with low repetitions and worked my way up. It was important that I didn't over-tire the muscles, because then I'd regress. The goal was to strengthen as many muscles as possible, but especially the ones that looked most promising and that would be most helpful in enabling me to walk. The whole apparatus fit in my bedroom, though it took up most of the space. We did my exercises for an hour in the morning, and for another hour at night. I did these exercises for a year.

I also started walking with a couple of canes. Mother or Daddy still had to help me to my feet and walk along with me, in case I stumbled or nearly fell. As time went by, I grew less nervous and more used to walking with canes.

Some of my new exercises were hard to do, and I'd get mad at Mother and Daddy. There for a while it seemed that I was constantly crying. I went through spells where I didn't know who to blame. It was just so discouraging, because progress was so slow. I was facing the fact that no matter how hard I worked, no matter how I wanted it, there were just going to be limits to what I could do physically. Even while I was crying, I was ashamed of myself.

To change the topic—big news—we bought a television set! I only watched one or two shows in the daytime, but at night I couldn't turn it off. *Art Linkletter's House Party* was a variety show. He'd host a guest, and have someone sing, and once in a while he'd go down the aisle, and have people sing with them. He always had three or four children who were six or seven years old, and he'd ask them questions. That segment was called "Kids Say the Darndest Things."

Years later, when I was about 26, I went with my friends Nadine and Bernice to California. Gordon got us tickets to the filming of the show.

Art Linkletter walked into the audience and asked who would like to spell a word for him. He picked Nadine, and she spelled "separate." She won a lawnmower. What was funny was that she'd go to dances, and as she'd be going out the door her mother would call after her, "Now be sure to tell the boys that you have your own lawnmower!"

November 1952 arrived, exactly one year since I contracted polio. As I look back on the year before, and consider all that has happened, I feel fortunate to be as far along physically as I am, even though there have been a lot of hard times. I am grateful that I have been able to feel the peace that I have. Looking back, I attribute that to my knowledge of my Heavenly Father, and the many times that I felt the Spirit. Added to that is the love and security I felt from my parents and my extended family and friends, as well as Gordon, when he got home from Korea. I have also been greatly blessed with an optimistic attitude. All this came together to help me be emotionally healthy, which is such an important part of life.

Just before Thanksgiving, Mother received a letter from Aunt Blanche telling her that Grandma had been awfully sick, and that she was going to the hospital to stay until she could be operated on two weeks later. Mother decided to fly to Seattle to be with Grandma for a few days, because they were afraid she might not survive the operation. Dad would take some leave days so he could stay home with me.

Thanksgiving Day arrived, and with it, a snowstorm. The airport phoned us, and asked Mother if it would be OK if she had a lay-over in Portland, and then flew on to Seattle the next day. Since Kent lived in Portland, Mother said that would be fine. So, then she could at least see him and Bernice, Melinda, and Kurt. We all took Mother to the airport and then went to Uncle Ralph's for Thanksgiving dinner and then to stay the night.

The next night, while we were in bed, Kathy brought the phone over and we called up "Moon Dial," a radio show. We asked the disc jockey if he'd dedicate a song to "Hard Clara," which was my old cast. "He'll probably play that awful song about the blue mountains that he plays every night," Kathy said, and guess what, he did! Oh well, what are you going to do?

The next morning, we returned home to Spanish Fork. Home seemed different without Mother. We did receive an air-mail letter from her. She had been at Kent's house, then Kent and Bernice had taken Mother to Seattle, but Mother didn't get to see Grandma until after the operation.

That next week passed slowly. I spent it doing my schoolwork. Daddy went to the office for a few hours every afternoon. Mother sent more letters, and we learned that Grandma wasn't doing well. Aunt Mae had also gone to Seattle, from San Francisco, to be there with her mother. The next Saturday, we received a letter saying that Grandma felt better, but that Mother had been down with the flu.

The next day, I made a cake and was just making the frosting when Aunt Edna and Uncle Stan and their two sons came by. They stayed for dinner, and then decided to spend the night with us. After dinner we watched television, and Aunt Edna kept making comments about how she couldn't get over what a good housekeeper Daddy was. That's because Uncle Stan had gotten the other side of the neatness genes. He was more like my grandpa, and didn't have much to do with keeping house.

We expected Mother home at any time. Dad had painted the kitchen since she'd left, and we'd kept it as a surprise for when she came back. Dad did the washing, and I did the ironing. One day both Gordon and Daddy had a white shirt in the wash. I was sitting, ironing Daddy's shirt, and Gordon came in and asked, "Is that my shirt?" He really looked pale. My Mother was a perfectionist, and so was Gordon, and I'd never ironed before. Gordon was worried I wouldn't do a good enough job.

"No," I said, "But I'll do yours next." I don't think that reassured him much.

That night, while I was doing my exercises, the phone rang. Daddy answered it and from his end of the conversation, I could tell that it was Mother, and that Grandma had passed away. When Daddy hung up, he confirmed what I already knew. He said we'd go to Salt Lake on Friday and meet Mother, Aunt Blanche, and Aunt Mae at the airport. The funeral would be held in Salt Lake City, which was really Grandma's home.

We went to the airport, but they weren't on the plane. We went to Uncle Ralph's, and he said that Mother had called, they had come on the midnight plane, and were at a hotel. We drove to the hotel, and I waited in the car while Daddy went up to their room to get them. After a bit, the door opened, and Mother came out, crying, with Aunt Mae and Aunt Blanche at her heels. Mother hugged me as if she'd been gone a year.

They got into the car, and as we drove away, they told us everything. It seems that Grandma had been doing very well, and then all at once she'd had a relapse, and that was it.

The funeral was on Tuesday. Before the casket was closed everyone went up to take a last look at Grandma. Everyone was sobbing, including me. I thought that Grandma looked very nice, especially considering all she'd been through. She was to be buried at Mt. Pleasant cemetery, 85 miles from Salt Lake City.

When we arrived home, everyone was there, and I remember us, all together, sitting around the dining room table, eating. My Mother's brothers, Sam and Leonard, didn't have much to say. My Mother's siblings were alcoholics, and a couple of them left that night to go and drink. I remember that Mother was upset that they'd gone out drinking the night they buried their mother.

Everyone left the next day. With Christmas less than a week and a half away, they had to get home. Mother went uptown to do some shopping, but everything was already picked over. That Friday we put up the Christmas tree. Dad made sure the lights worked, and he put them on the tree. Mother had to put on the garland. She was the only one who knew how to do it. She wouldn't do anything else, but she had to see that the garland was just so. Then Dad and I put on the ornaments, and I remember that we had Christmas music on in the background. Everyone put the long, thin, metallic icicles on their trees then, and they looked nice if you took your time doing them.

I remember the companionable feeling, working with Dad to decorate the tree that Christmas, and every Christmas before that, as well. I remember him telling me about his Christmases when he was younger.

Dad said that when he was growing up they didn't put the tree up until Christmas Eve. Their home was a typical house, built at the turn of the century. They had a parlor, with a piano. When I was growing up, I'd sometimes go into that parlor to play the piano. The parlor was always cold because they heated their house with a heater-olla. A heater-olla was basically a small furnace or a stove, four or five feet tall that stood on four short legs. It had a door in the front, and you'd put wood and coal in it, and light it, and the heat would come out of vents in the sides. There was one in the parlor, and another in the dining room, and a coal cook-stove in the kitchen.

After we had the tree up, Dad said that he needed Gordon's help over in the Forest office lot warehouse. For Christmas, I'd asked for a bookcase for my bedroom, and for a typewriter. I wanted the bookcase because I'd received a lot of gifts from people, knick-knacks, storybook dolls, and such, and I wanted to display them along with my books. I assume that Dad wanted Gordon's help with the bookcase over in the warehouse.

Janet came over Christmas Eve with a gift for me, and I gave her the present I'd gotten her. After she'd gone home, I got down on the floor to feel her present through the wrapping to see if I could figure out what it was, even though she'd told me not to. I spent most of my time on the floor re-arranging the gifts, and snooping at the ones that were for me.

Christmas Eve, the florist sent some roses and a letter. The delivery girl who brought them said that she wasn't supposed to tell us who sent them, but she told us, anyway. They were from an older man from Dad's hometown. He was a writer who wrote short stories and such. He'd written a wonderful letter of encouragement to me. He told me of his admiration for me, which bothered me, because he didn't know that I yelled at my parents.

The holidays were over, and I was back to the same old grind again. I didn't go out much, though almost every Saturday night I went over to Janet's house. I was able to get myself up and out of chairs by then. This was a big deal for me, and in my eyes, a huge improvement, though I think I noticed it more than anyone else did.

I felt more independent, and sometimes I felt that Daddy wanted to help me too much, and I'd get angry. Each time I started to get up off a chair, either he or Mother would say, "What do you want? Can't I get it for you?" This upset me, because they'd said that I should walk more, but then I realized that I demanded a lot from them, too.

Once, my friend Janet invited me to go bowling and my mother took her in the kitchen and scolded her for doing so, saying how could she do that knowing that Myrna would never be able to bowl again. Janet surprised herself when she told off my mother by saying, "Myrna needs to get out of the house, her friends want her to be with them, and maybe she can't bowl but she can keep score and spend time with her friends." Mother let me go with them and I did initially keep score and chat with my friends, but eventually I wanted to try to bowl. So, with my left hand holding onto someone, I held the ball in my right hand and rolled it down the lane.

It was the middle of February, and I started counting the days left that my cast had to be on. Dr. Clegg had said that we would probably be able to take it off in May, which would make thirteen months in all that I had worn a cast.

I got a new therapist, and we went to work with him every other week. He was teaching me how to use a certain muscle in my left thigh, and then one day, I was able to move it. I was so happy. However, it never did get strong enough to actually move my leg. All it could ever do was make my leg twitch a little bit.

Dr. Clegg had been to a convention, and had gotten an idea for an exercise board that he wanted Dad to make because they weren't available for sale yet. Daddy went into Salt Lake to see the example of it and then he made me one like it. It was a big board that Daddy attached to one end of my existing exercise equipment. I stood on a board that teetered to one side and then the other. I was strapped to the big board behind my back, and I moved my legs up and down to build the muscles that hike the legs up and down, so I could strengthen my walking muscles. I started out doing this for a half hour every day, usually in the afternoon. I listened to the radio and sang along with a popular music station to help the time go by.

I went outside quite a bit and practiced walking with my two canes without anyone to help me, although it worried my parents for me to do so. They had good reason to worry, as I could've buckled so easily and gone down.

The teacher of my church young women's group, "Mia Maids" as it was called, came by, and said that if I wanted, I could graduate that year if I was willing to work for it. I jumped at the chance and I passed all the requirements, but I couldn't get into church with all the stairs to give my talk, so we decided to hold a "Fireside Chat" at home instead. I gave a book review of *Added Upon*. It was about the idea that you're born and you die, and depending on what you've done, you have blessings added upon you. We all had an enjoyable evening.

About the middle of April, when I only had three more weeks until my cast would come off, we went to Ephraim for a weekend. I went over to Uncle Stan's house in the afternoon. We had supper there, and then I went over to my aunt's house to stay the night. I walked into the kitchen and got a drink and was standing with my back against the sink holding onto my canes, when all of a sudden, I buckled and fell hard. I was standing on a throw rug, and when I moved it had slipped just a tiny bit, threw me off balance, and down I went. My legs hurt for a few minutes, but then just my right ankle hurt.

I had fallen in February, and had gotten right up again, so I thought that this was just the same kind of fall, but it wasn't. I started to shake, not with cold, but from the shock. Aunt VaLene kept encouraging me to get up, and trying to help me, but I was shaking too much. So, she covered me with a blanket, and I lay there until I calmed down a little.

About an hour later, Mother came, and I decided I could crawl to the couch and then get up on my feet from there. My ankle was sore when I tried to walk on it, and my knees hurt a little. I got in bed, and after I did, I felt better, and I stopped shaking. I had a bad night, though. My right leg hurt, and I had to keep taking aspirin. The next morning, I decided to try sitting up. I'd been awake for more than an hour, and I just had to get up. There was a chair at the end of the bed, so I walked, holding onto the chair, and then sat down.

Soon after, VaLene got up and put my foot in some hot water, which helped. Later, Dad came over and wrapped it up. That helped, too, though my foot still hurt. VaLene remembered that she had some pills left over from when her son Russell had a tooth pulled, and she gave me one, which made me feel a whole lot better.

Mother, Dad and I left for home in the middle afternoon. That night I had to take a sleeping pill to sleep. I woke up Monday morning, and went only as far as the couch. My knees and ankle still ached, so Mother hot-packed them. I slept all morning, but was conscious of Mother putting on and taking off the packs.

Tuesday, I was sore all through my chest and back. Mother called the doctor at noon, but he couldn't come over until after five. Then Mother started hot-packing me all over. We thought that I must have wrenched my back and chest when I fell. Mother took my temperature, and it was over 100, so she thought I had the three-day measles that were going around. When the doctor arrived, and examined me, he said I had pneumonia! He gave me pills and cough medicine. Since then, I've learned that often when a person falls, it's a shock to the body and lowers the body's resistance. Older people, especially, will often come down with pneumonia after a fall.

The next day I didn't feel very sick, and I coughed only once, so I guessed I didn't have pneumonia very badly. I was very weak, and the doctor wouldn't even let me put my feet on the floor, so I lay and listened to the radio. People called to see how my measles were. Don't ask me how that rumor got started! By Saturday, I felt well enough to get up.

Carol had been coming over to visit, and she always brought her knitting, so I decided that I'd let her show me how to knit, too. I started a pair of stockings for Gordon, and it was a lot of fun. I doubt that he ever wore them, though I hope he appreciated my effort.

Then the time came for them to take off my cast. I'd been counting the seconds until my cast could come off, but when it came down to it, I was really nervous. I think I was afraid that they'd find they had to put another one back on.

Dr. Clegg's nurse sawed off the cast. It felt like someone had taken the body right out of me. I was so used to it supporting me, and now, suddenly, that was gone. I had to take hold of Daddy's arm to even walk to the X-ray room, I was so weak. We'd brought the corset that I'd worn before the cast, and once that was back on, I felt more secure. I still couldn't walk with my canes, though. It felt like they were made of wobbly rubber.

The next day, I got in the bathtub for the first time in thirteen months. Whenever I'm supposed to tell something unusual about myself, or play the game, "Two Truths and a Lie," I always say that one time I went for over a year without taking either a shower or a bath. I stayed in the tub for an hour, until Mother made me get out. Getting in and out was a lot easier than it had been before. I sat on the toilet, made a quarter turn and put my legs into the tub. Then, using my arms to guide me down, I lowered myself onto the side of the bathtub, and then down into the water.

I got out all my clothes that I hadn't been able to wear for so long, and tried them all on. Nothing fit—not one dress, or one skirt. Everything was too tight; I'd grown in the past year. It made me sick, that four dresses and five skirts had to be put away because they didn't fit any more, and I hadn't even been able to wear them. I'd bought them for school the autumn before I got polio. On Monday I made myself a skirt so I'd have something to wear.

My teachers continued taking me through my schoolwork, and by the middle of May I was pretty much done. I'd also been working on memorizing two piano pieces for a recital. They were "The Spinning Song" by Mendelsohn, and "Valise in C-sharp Minor," by Chopin. I deeply loved my pieces. I was beginning to really love the piano.

We'd be able to go to Ephraim for Memorial Day that year, so I made myself a new sleeveless dress out of red tissue gingham with a full skirt and a V neck. I made a little white jacket to go with it.

By Memorial Day, I was able to walk on my own with two canes, though not very well. I was bent clear over, because I was so weak from relying on the cast to support me for so long. I felt like a piece of rubber. To my delight, it was a nice day for Memorial Day. I walked around the cemetery holding onto Nedra's and Linda's hands. We had a lot of fun, as always.

At church, I went to the "Tying of the Rose Bouquet" program. That was how we graduated from the Young Women's Mia Maids class. I chose a red rose and said that it represented Faith, and that I thought we needed more faith in the world. I had a hard time walking up to put the rose in the vase, but I managed it. Afterward, we had our pictures taken. The photographer forgot to put film in his camera, so we all had to come back a week later and have the picture taken over again. I stood in the middle and held two girls' hands, and when we got the pictures you wouldn't notice that I was being supported by them.

Myrna front and center in the 'Tying of the Rose Bouquet' program

The following Sunday, I played in Helen's recital. I didn't play as well as I wanted to. Mr. Reese, who had taught me how to play the cello in the eighth grade, came up to me and told me that he'd thought I'd played well. He said that I should keep up the good work. The fact that my balance had improved so that I was able to sit on the piano bench and not a chair helped me to play better. His comment made me feel really good, because I hadn't had a particularly positive experience with him when I'd played the cello in school.

The fall before eighth grade, Mr. Reese asked me if I would play the cello for the school orchestra because they were desperate for someone. His argument was that there wasn't much call for a piano player, and when an orchestra did need a pianist, most often a guest pianist came in for a special performance. He said that I would get more of a chance to play if I took up the cello, so I reluctantly did. I didn't practice very much because I didn't like carrying the huge cello in its case back and forth from school to home, and I didn't take private lessons, either. I learned to read the notes enough to play the strings, but certainly not very well. The thing I liked best about being in orchestra was when the ninth-grade girl who did play the piano was absent, I got to fill in for her. At the beginning of ninth grade Mr. Reese was still so desperate for a cello player that even the principal called me down to his office and pleaded with me to stay with it for another year. But I told him that if I were to spend time practicing, I wanted to focus on the piano, and not the cello.

Towards the end of the year Janet took my yearbook with her to school and had people sign it for me. Most of them said pretty much the same thing, "Hope you get better soon, I miss you, have a good summer." The point, of course, was getting lots of signatures and filling up the end pages. My English teacher, Miss Wilkinson, wrote, "It has been fun visiting with you, and it has been an inspiration to partake of your cheerful spirit. May you continue to keep this optimism as you continue to improve and grow in body and in spirit."

Another person who wrote in my yearbook was Jeneel, a good friend I'd had since I was five years old. She and her mother and her brother lived around the corner with her grand-parents. I remember the afternoon she called and invited me over. My mother put my coat on me, instructing me that I should keep my coat on, since I had a hole in my dress. Of course, the first thing Jeneel said to me was, "Can I take your coat?" and without hesitation, I handed it right over.

She wrote in my yearbook: "We've really had fun all these years we've known each other. Golly, we had to have fun after the riot of a way that we met. Remember all the fun we had in grade school, despite the little fights we had sometimes? Good friends have to learn to fight once in a while. Remember how we used to hint around for a date? Remember the Halloween dance when we got scared out of our wits? Remember how we played house down in your basement? I could never forget all the fun we had. You'll go a long way in life."

Though I knew how much I missed my friends at school, I hadn't really thought of how they might miss me, but when I read what Janet wrote, "Here's to one of the sweetest people I know. You are really a girl with a lot of spunk. Myrna, you'll never know how much I've missed you since you've been out of school. I've really enjoyed having you for a friend and neighbor. I hope that we'll always be friends," it made me realize that it went both ways.

CHAPTER 11

Summer of 1953

Towards the end of my sophomore year I was facing a long summer without anything to do except my exercises. Daddy went to someone he knew at the bank, and asked him if there was something I could do to occupy my time. The man gave Daddy a document that he wanted typed up. It was about eight or ten pages long with three carbon copies behind each page. I was typing three copies at once. I hadn't much experience with it, and I got so frustrated because I would make a mistake, and then have to go through each of the copies and correct it. On one page, I made so many mistakes that if I didn't cry, I sure wanted to.

Gordon felt sorry for me, so he sat down and typed a few pages. Finally, I finished it, and Daddy took it back to the guy at the bank. Evidently my typing course at home hadn't been as demanding as it would have been at school, and I decided that I'd wait until I had more experience before I tried typing something like that again!

Gordon had gotten a job selling aluminum awnings that summer. The company he worked for suggested that he get a tape recorder and practice his sales pitch into it. He'd listen to himself and learn to critique his speech and style. Tape recorders were different then than they are now. The tape recorder that he bought was one and a half feet long, at least one foot wide, and another high. It had two reels on the top and plugged into the wall. It was a big piece of machinery.

I also used the tape recorder. I was trying to learn shorthand, and in the shorthand textbook there would be a paragraph. After so many words there would be a mark that indicated to the teacher how fast to read it. The ultimate goal, after two years of taking short-hand, was to be able to take down 120 words per minute.

Every day I worked on English and typing and shorthand. I'd also practice the piano and read. I began to read the classics and books that were of higher quality. This was when I started to develop a greater appreciation for quality literature, and when I started to have a real love for books. My English teacher would bring me books, and so would my friends. Mother and Dad signed up for a book club where they received a book in the mail every few months, and I'd read them. I read Jane Eyre and I really liked it. I cried and cried when I read she became an orphan, was put into an orphanage, and how cruel they were to her.

I did embroidery and crocheting that summer, and Carol tried to teach me to knit, but I didn't pick that up very well. We went to drive-in movies, as that was one of the ways that I could get out of the house.

Another thing that helped pass time that summer was that my friends would come and play games with me. Janet came over a lot, and so did Bernice, who lived a block and a half west of us. We played board games, but we mainly played Rook and Canasta.

My lifelong friend Bernice

I started to go swimming, both because I wanted to go for the exercise and to build up strength. Daddy took me in the first time. I couldn't even move in the water. I had to hold my legs down with my hands to begin with. I didn't feel like I had control of my body like I did before, but slowly, with Dad's help, I began to do better. I wasn't afraid of the water because I'd always liked to swim, even before I'd gotten polio. Soon I got to a point where I could hang onto the side of the pool with my hands and stretch out on my stomach, and move my legs behind me a little bit. Not long after that I was able to let go altogether and doggy-paddle around.

I soon got to a point to where Dad felt that others could take me swimming. Gordon took me over sometimes, and Carol would take me once or twice a week in the evenings after she got home from work. I could get from the car and to the pool by holding onto her arm with one hand and grasping a cane in the other. Then I'd get into the water by hanging onto the railing, like I'd go down the steps at home.

Carol was a great friend in that she was willing to go to the trouble to take me after a long day at work, and she was also a lot of fun. We could talk about anything. In those days, you were supposed to wait an hour after eating to go swimming, so we'd be hungry when we were done. Most of the time we'd stop at the drive-in and have dinner, just the two of us with money that Mother had provided.

There were two swimming pools in the area, but the one I liked better was Park Rochet in the north part of Springville. It was just a nicer pool all around. I was gradually able to move my legs more and more in the water. I'm sure that swimming that summer, as well as the other exercises I was doing at home helped me to develop the muscles that I needed to prepare my legs for the surgery that was planned for later.

I was working even harder with my weights, and continually pushed myself to do more repetitions and with heavier weights. Some of my muscles were becoming stronger and stronger, but others didn't seem to make much progress. I religiously did my exercises at least five times a week. In the morning I'd do the weights, in the afternoon I'd do the teeter-totter, and in the evening Dad would stretch my legs and we'd do resistance work against his pushing. I also went walking every day. We'd go outside if the weather was good, and if it wasn't, we'd walk around inside the house. I stayed busy.

I had gotten to the point where I did most of my walking without the brace but with canes. I wanted to become as independent of any mechanical contrivance as I could. I also felt that I could build up my muscles more when I went without the brace because I could bend and flex my leg farther.

Over time, I was able to get around with my canes as well as I had before my cast was removed. I could go up the few steps to the house alone by holding one cane in the hand I used on the railing, while using the other cane in the other hand to support me as I went up. But I still couldn't take those two steps in front of the dresser when getting out of bed. It seemed like I couldn't put my weight on my right hip. If only my right hip were as strong as my left one. Looking back, I think it was that my left foot was so much stronger than the right foot, and so I could control my whole leg so much better, where my right foot would go out to the side with every step, and I had less control over it.

Walking with two canes and no cast

Towards the end of June, I decided to go to Ephraim and spend a whole week with Nedra. I knew that Mother would worry the whole time I was gone, but I figured that she needed to get used to me being more independent, and to learn not to worry. Before I went, I made some more clothes so I'd have something to wear.

Mother and Dad took me to Ephraim on Sunday, and then went back home that same night. I had a nice time visiting. Nedra worked almost every day for eight hours, but during that time I played and talked to Suzanne. The nights Nedra had dates, I talked with Charles. Rue was up in the mountains with the sheep. I teased Nedra about all her boyfriends and wondered out loud if she was ever going to get serious.

If I were honest, I felt a little homesick. That was first time since I'd had polio that I hadn't had Mother or Dad there every minute to help me get dressed or with whatever else I needed. To help Mother, (or was it to help me?) I wrote three post-cards home to her in that one week. I gave the first one to Aunt Edna to mail for me, but later in the week I noticed that it was still on top of the fridge. Mother didn't get that one, but she did get the other two, so at least I didn't look as pathetic as I could have.

Back in the summer of 1949 Gordon had worked at the pipe plant that was between Springville and Provo. While he was working there, he met a guy who became a friend. He would take this friend flying in his Cessna. Towards the end of the summer this friend suggested that Gordon quit the pipe plant a couple weeks earlier than he was planning to and go up to Wyoming with him to round up some wild horses. He thought that Gordon could fly up and use the Cessna to help the guys on the ground herd and corral the horses. Gordon jumped at the chance. His pay would be one of the horses, and Gordon picked out this little wild sorrel. He named it Cheyenne.

The friend helped Gordon truck the horse down to Spanish Fork, and there Gordon boarded the horse in a pasture. Every day when Gordon came home from the University, the first thing he would do was change clothes and fill his pockets with sugar cubes and carrots. Then he went out and began the process of taming Cheyenne. He had sugar cubes in his hand and walked up to the horse. At first Cheyenne was really shy, but after a while he became less and less shy, and then finally he would eat the sugar and carrots out of Gordon's hand. Then he'd let Gordon pet him, and then put a rope around his neck to lead him around the corral, and eventually he tolerated Gordon putting a blanket on his back. Then Gordon progressed to putting a bridle on Cheyenne. Once Gordon thought the horse was ready to be ridden, he got his friend, Cleve, to go with him to the corral to hold the reins while Gordon got on the horse. Everything went well.

Besides Cheyenne, there were other horses Dad kept at the station. These horses were owned by the government. Dad would take up the horse of a friend, Nate Hales, so the horse could get more exercise than he'd get just standing in the pasture all day. Dad called the horse Old Nate, and before Cheyenne came along, I liked riding him best because he was gentle and easy to handle. He was the horse that I rode the most in my younger years.

The horse that Dad rode the most was Tony Deluxe. All of Dad's horses had the name "Tony." The summer before I got polio Dad had a government horse that he rode that he named "Tony Holly." I don't know why he liked "Tony" so much. I liked how Tony Holly picked up his feet and how he liked to go fast. The horse I learned to gallop on was Snake Eye. He was a black horse, but he had a white mark that looked like the S-curve of a snake between his eyes. He was a bit wild.

We were planning to have a family reunion around the first of August up at Strawberry. I decided to write Dr. Clegg and ask him if I could go horseback riding. Mother said it was just a waste of paper, she knew I couldn't go horseback riding this soon after my cast was taken off. I wrote anyway and I got an immediate answer. It said that after the first of September I could go horse-back riding. "Well, we will go up to Strawberry again for Labor Day and then I will be able to ride the horses." I was really satisfied!

The next time we went to Strawberry, my legs were stronger, and I was looking forward to riding Cheyenne. I wasn't sure how I was going to get on, but I was sure that Daddy would figure out a way.

My first ride on Cheyenne after having polio

He put the truck tailgate down and lifted me up into the back of the truck and then got up in the bed with me. I stood there with my canes while Mother led Cheyenne up alongside the back of the truck, and then Daddy lifted me into the saddle. He had the stirrups up so that my feet could fit into them. I took hold of the horn with one hand, and the reins with the other, and we took off.

Oh, what a wonderful feeling, to be back in the saddle again! I didn't have much strength in my right leg to kick or nudge him with, but I could nudge him a little with my left leg. It was enough to have him walk. Dad would say, "Make him walk up," which meant to make him walk faster. Gordon had done a fine job training Cheyenne, but Dad said he was too tame, because he walked so slowly.

At first Dad and I would ride around the pasture, which was about as large as two city blocks. I got used to riding again, and we'd ride farther each day. There was still the problem of Cheyenne walking so slowly. One day, Dad had a bright idea. He remembered that in the garage next to the cabin there were the stirrups that Gordon and Kent had used as little boys. He strapped them around my ankles, and they gave Cheyenne enough incentive to walk at just the right pace, not so fast that I wasn't in control, but not so slow that Dad was unhappy.

Just being up to Strawberry was wonderful. Sitting at the table and looking out the window at the lake was so peaceful. That is one of the most precious moments in my life, and one that I will always remember. I think back on it from time to time, and take comfort from the calming, peaceful feeling that I had then. It felt as if everything was right with the world. I can still smell the sweet scent of the horses, which was a combination of their hay-filled droppings and their sun-warmed, faintly sweaty coats. There was also the fresh smell of the earth after the rain had stopped.

One day Mother and Dad and I went out on the lake in a row boat. We went along the one side of the lake where Dad knew of good places to catch fish, where the Bryant Fork River flowed into the lake. Dad dropped the anchor and we sat there, calmly waiting, when suddenly there was a jerk on my fishing pole. Since I couldn't stand up, Dad got up to help me wind in the reel, and we pulled in a beautiful trout, that believe it or not, was nearly nineteen inches long and weighed three and a half pounds!

With the big fish I'd caught!

Shortly after we got it pulled in a wind came up. Dad pulled in the anchor, and we headed towards shore. The lake got really rough, and for a minute there, I wondered if we might not go overboard, but I knew in the same moment that my Dad would never let that happen. Of course, we made it to shore just fine.

CHAPTER 12

Surgery After Surgery

One beautiful Sunday towards the end of October, I was going down the front steps without my brace when my right knee buckled, and down I went. Dad picked me up. My knee was very sore, so he carried me into the house and laid me down on the sofa. My knee began to swell up, and kept hurting, so Mother gave me some aspirin, but it didn't help. Mother thought we should call the doctor, but Dad and I thought that it was just pulled or strained, as it wasn't swollen that much. So, Dad carried me into the bedroom and Mother helped me into bed, and I spent a very miserable night as the aspirin did nothing for the pain. I didn't sleep much. Dad lay down by me so that Mother could sleep, and so he could keep an eye on me and help me with anything he could, but there wasn't much he could do. It was a painful night.

The next morning Dad took me over to the hospital. An X-ray showed that I had a hair-line fracture right above the knee joint. The doctor put on a full-leg cast and wrote a prescription for pain pills, and with the two I was finally able to get some relief. I also found myself back in a wheelchair. It had an extension on the right foot peg to hold my leg straight out.

With my right leg in a cast

After wearing the cast for seven weeks, the leg was finally healed enough that I could have the cast removed. It really took me by surprise at how painful it was to bend my leg after having it straight out for all that time. I had to gradually bend my leg over the next couple of days, but by then it was back to normal. After that I went back to my full routine with my school work and walking, piano-playing, and all my exercises. I felt strongly about doing all my exercises every day so my muscles could get as strong as possible before the transplant surgeries that I knew were coming up the next summer. I needed that much time to build them up, but looking back now, I think that Dr. Clegg figured that by then I would've gone as far, physically, as I was likely to go.

At the beginning of April, the next year, Dad traded in our 1948 Plymouth and bought a brand-new car—a 1954 Pontiac. It was a light sky-blue on the top and white on the bottom. That was a popular color scheme that year. Like all kids, I was excited that Dad brought home a new car, but what really excited me the most was that the Pontiac was an automatic, and didn't have a clutch. Mother, Dad, and I were hopeful that without having to use a clutch, I would eventually be able to drive. I might be able to use one foot for the brake and the other for the gas.

The middle of April, Mother and Dad and I went on a road trip. My brother Kent lived in Portland, Oregon. We thought we'd go up to see him and his wife Bernice and their two kids, Melinda, who was about five, and Kurt, who was two. Mother's sister Blanche, her husband Ed, and their daughter Roxanna lived near Seattle, and we planned to go visit them, as well.

We began our trip by going north through McCall, Idaho. It was surprising to me how high the snow was there. It was as high as the windows in our motel. We visited Mother's sister-in-law, Goldie, at her coffee shop. Goldie and Mom's brother, Leonard, were divorced. I don't know about anything else she cooked, but Goldie's hamburgers and fries were the best I had ever tasted! She was a fun-loving, happy person, and it was a pleasure to be around her. Leonard later came to Aunt Blanche's and spent an evening with us. It was nice to see him.

Then we went to Kent's home in Portland. We spent some time sightseeing, but mostly we just spent time with my brother and his wife and the kids, getting to know them and letting them get to know us.

Our visit with Kent, wife and kids in Oregon

Kent was in real estate. He bought low cost houses, and had taught himself to fix them up and sell them for a profit. He did quite well that way. He had always been very ambitious and a go-getter. He had figured ways to make money even when he was just a kid. He delivered papers till he was fifteen or so, and then Gordon took over his route. In those days, in the late 30's the movie theater sold candy bars, but they didn't sell popcorn or drinks. Kent made popcorn in the drugstore next door to the Spanish Fork movie theater. He suggested to the owner of the drugstore that he put the popcorn machine out on the sidewalk in front of the movie theater so he could sell more popcorn, and he did!

When we got home I had some catching-up to do with schoolwork. I also needed to prepare two piano pieces. The Utah Federation of Music Clubs sponsored a musical festival in Spanish Fork for piano students. The students came from Springville, Spanish Fork and Payson. My teacher, Helen Hawkins, had me play pieces that were below my ability in the hope that I would be more likely to receive a Superior rating, and consequently, I did.

The festival was held in the Union Building at the University of Utah in early May. I will always remember how peaceful I felt as I gazed over the top of the grand piano as I performed my selection. The whole day was a wonderful experience, and I might add, with a great lunch!

While all of this was going on I continued with my daily exercises in anticipation of the surgeries scheduled for the first part of June. My parents and I had worked hard at my exercises for the past two and a half years. We and Dr. Clegg all felt that I had developed all the strength in my muscles that I was ever going to be able to. Now was the time to see if all the exercises I'd done would pay off.

We arrived at the LDS Hospital on a Friday afternoon for the surgeries. I was assigned a room with four beds. There were people in the other two beds, but no one was in the bed beside me. My blood was drawn, my temperature, blood pressure, and heart rate and other such pre-operative procedures were done.

The next morning I was awakened at 6 a.m. and given all the usual shots that just made me go back to sleep. The next thing I remember was waking up in the very same bed. I was happily surprised when I realized that the operation was over, and I had very little pain. What a difference compared to two years before, when I'd had such excruciating pain with my back surgery!

My cast this time went from near the base of my toes up to right below my knee. Because my right big toe was so strong, the doctor pulled the muscle out of that toe and moved it to the center of my foot. On the top of my big toe the doctor took five stitches. He took another five or so stitches on the top of my foot about in the middle of my arch. On the bottom of my foot, almost to the inside edge of my foot, were about three stitches. That was the first surgery.

The muscle that moved my right foot to the right was very strong. The doctor made a small incision and took that muscle and moved it up almost completely over my ankle. That was the second surgery. Then Dr. Clegg made an incision on the outside and below my ankle, and lifted the tissue from off the bone and fused it so that my ankle was stabilized and was straight, rather than canted to one side. With all this working together, once everything healed, hopefully I would be able to partially lift my foot up and then be able to put it back down. That was Saturday's round of surgeries.

Although I have never understood how Dr. Clegg attached muscles here and there and to what, I just had faith that he knew what he was doing. The pain was never very bad.

The next morning the nurse came in and gave me a shot to put me back to sleep for the next operation. I took a couple of flowers out of the vase to smell them and was holding them on my chest when I went to sleep. When Mother and Dad came in, Mother had quite a shock, because there I was, looking like I was lying dead with flowers in my hands. Doctor Clegg met me by the elevator and had me tighten the muscles of both my legs so he could make a last-minute check of which leg still needed surgery.

When I woke up I was back in my room. My cast now completely covered from the top of my right leg to the tip of my toes. The cast on my left leg went from the top of my leg down to the ankle. The doctor had taken the hamstring on the outside of my left leg and separated it and pulled one half from underneath my knee to the top of my knee. Then he did the same thing with the other half of the split hamstring on the inside of my leg, and in so doing made long incisions on either side of my leg. I had over 100 stitches on my legs and foot.

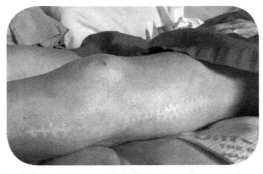

Scars I had throughout my life from muscle transplant surgeries

On my right leg, the hamstring on the inside was too weak to use, but on the outside Dr. Clegg did a similar surgery as he'd done on my left leg. The pain I experienced then was worse than after my foot surgery, but not nearly as bad as after my back surgery. However, I was having a hard time sleeping because I couldn't get comfortable.

My father had gone home on Wednesday to work, and came back Friday evening. He and Mother were staying at Aunt Erma's. I couldn't sleep that night, and at 6 a.m. I was so worn out emotionally that I called, knowing that Dad would answer the phone. He came right over to the hospital to be with me. There wasn't much he could do, but it was comforting just to have him there.

Dr. Clegg came in at nine and said that I could go home. That was really a surprise. We'd thought I'd need to be at the hospital longer. He got a kick out of my painted toenails below my cast. My cousins Kathy and Linda had painted them at my request the day before when they came to visit.

Arriving home with casts on both legs after muscle transplant surgeries

At home, Dad had taken down the dining room table and put it in my bedroom. Then, in the dining room, he'd set up a single bed. It would have been impossible for me to turn into my bedroom from the hall in my wheelchair with both my legs sticking straight out in their casts. I slept in the dining room for the next two months.

A little over two weeks after the surgeries I began to feel the new muscles on my legs. Several weeks later the cast on my left leg was removed but my right foot was still not healed and they had to put a new cast on it. By September of 1954, twelve weeks after my surgeries, all my casts had been removed.

Dr. Clegg demonstrated how to use the muscles and provided me with exercises to do alone and to have others do with me. As the days went by I could gradually lift my legs higher and control them. We had thought that my right food would still require a brace even though it had been fused straight during the operation, yet it healed so well that Dr. Clegg said I would not need one. I was so happy!

With the arrival of September came the departure of Gordon again. He had received a fellowship to study at New York University in Manhattan. We were sure going to miss him, but we were also thankful that he had this opportunity. It served him very well, as Gordon would later become a very successful retail businessman, serving as the CEO of various companies.

A week before school started Dad and I went to meet with the principal to talk about the classes I would take and how things would work for my senior year. I was really hoping to be able to attend school this year but obviously, I wasn't going to be able to until I could fully get up on my feet again. The following week teachers began visiting me at home as they had the previous years.

I had started to walk with Dad or Mother's arm and then one crutch in the other hand. The day after my birthday in September, I was waiting for Dad to come and help me into supper and I looked at the crutches and noticed they were within reach, so I took them and successfully walked to the kitchen without any help. This made me happy because I had been in a morbid mood all day. Mother had been in bed sick and I was alone without help to move. For the first time since I had polio I had wondered if I would ever walk again. This went on until suddenly, like a flash, I remembered the blessing that I had been given by Apostle Harold B. Lee. I felt completely lifted again and filled with hope.

October 1954 after all casts had been removed

The therapist told us that the best exercise for me would be to practice standing and moving between parallel bars and to use a stationary bicycle. By the end of that week Daddy had made some parallel bars and put them in my bedroom. The first time I used them I was able to stand for 7 seconds, a week later I was able to stand up alone for 4 minutes! Then, I started walking with just one hand on the bars.

I could put all my weight on my left leg and swing my right leg forward like a pendulum, grabbing on to the bar for support. Then I got to where I could put my right leg forward and then bring my left leg forward by bending over, not grabbing the bars. So, there I was standing with my arms way back and bent in a 90-degree angle. While standing, I slowly straightened myself and did the same thing again, taking hold of the bars in between. I practiced this secretly for two weeks and then showed my parents. My pattern was step, step, bend, straighten, take hold of bar and repeat. After another week or so I got so that by throwing my weight to one side I didn't need to bend as much but I was still twisting my body a lot. I continued practicing for weeks.

Though I didn't get out much, I certainly went out a lot in my dreams. No kidding. A lot of my dreams were of me in school, sometimes with my crutches or canes and sometimes just walking. I was sure hoping this would come true. I was also wishing that I could go out with boys, just sometimes.

That November I was able to attend a banquet at the church for the youth. The leader, Mr. Whitehead, said how happy he was to see me there and mentioned that just last week one of the youth, while saying prayer, had prayed that I could be at their banquet. This startled me for a minute. Then, I got thinking, "I wonder how many other times people have prayed certain things for me, when I have done it without thinking that the Lord or anyone else had much to do with it. This certainly gave me greater faith.

At the same time, I guess I got pretty mean sometimes to my parents. I didn't hit, yell or cry, but was just snotty and sassy! I kept thinking I was going to be nicer but then…boom! I'd say something I shouldn't. One day Mother told me off. It did me good and I think I improved after that. I hope so.

At Christmas time, Dad took us to the stores shopping. He would take me on one arm and I would have a cane in the other. By this time, I was walking by myself using a cane in one hand and a crutch in the other, but by New Year's I was using just two canes. We visited Dr. Clegg and my therapist Dr. Green in January and they both agreed that I should start learning to walk with just one cane. So, I immediately tried but it seemed effortless. I held one cane in my hand without putting it on the floor and tried walking with only the other cane in my other hand. It was very difficult and being so it was very hard on my nerves. I realized, that I had come to a place now, where I had to build up a new muscle. This was a different kind of muscle, and one that would need a lot of work done on it. It was called 'moral support.' My therapist agreed, that one couldn't just say, "I am going to do this," and do it. It just wasn't that easy. It would take time and practice.

On January 4, 1955, I attended school in person for the first time since getting polio. We had figured out that I could attend school twice a week, participating in sewing class, because it was easy to get to and didn't require steps. Dad or Mother would drive me there and pick me up later. After sewing, I would then go to the sick room where I would study alone and the teachers who used to come to the house would come there to give me my instructions. Even though I was in a small room behind a shut door, it gave me a thrill to hear the students in the hall when the bell rang. I was, at least, a little part of the routine of school. Another thrill was attending three high school basketball games that season. The principal gave me a seat right next to the pep team, where I could get in easily and really get into the spirit of the game.

One day, it had rained so much that the entrance I used to get in the school was flooded, so Daddy, against my will, carried me into the main door of the school and down a flight of stairs.

Every afternoon that I was at school, someone different would come in to see me. One day, Mr. Finley, the chorus teacher, visited me and said he had heard that I played the piano and would I like to play a solo at the school music festival. I was naturally pleased at the opportunity. About this time, I started leaving the door to my little room open. Then I could see and say hello to the students going into chorus. Every now and then someone would come in and talk to me as if they knew me and I would have to look them up that night in my yearbook to find out who they were.

One of the other students who participated in the music festival was Richard Christiansen. The day after the festival was Friday, and after the last bell rang he happened to see me as he passed my door. There was a girl with him but she left. I guess it was because he kept talking with me. He was still there when Mother came to get me. Saturday afternoon I came inside after practicing walking with Dad and Mother said, "Guess who wants to take you to a show tonight?" I didn't know, but had a feeling it might be Richard. Then, to my surprise, I was right. Mother went on to say that he had asked her if she thought he could handle me and she said she would leave it up to me. So, he said he would call back. He did, and I naturally said yes. He ended the conversation with, "thank you." I thought to myself, "thank me? Thank you!!!" That was my first date in over three years. I had often wondered who would be my first date. I didn't think it would be anyone that I had known for only two days.

Grandpa Nielson has been staying with us because he wasn't well. Even though quite deaf, he had taken everything in and he kept saying, "you're going, aren't you?" About six thirty, he said, "it looks like your partner's forgotten. But, of course, I don't know what time the matinee starts here." Good old grandpa. He was really happy to see me go out. Later, when I looked back on that evening, I was grateful to Richard for asking me out if it was just for grandpa's sake. I discovered later that Grandpa told all the relatives that I had a courtier.

When Richard arrived, I introduced him to grandpa. Daddy had planned to have a talk with him, but all he said was, "be careful." I guess my parents were really going through something. Their little girl, who had held on to them so much these past few years, was beginning her first steps in getting wings a little bit away from their ties.

Richard took me to the movie in town and after we drove around the city. When we got home we played the piano and talked until after twelve thirty. He was easy to talk with and I thought I liked him. But he didn't trill me. We went out a few more times but he also had eyes for someone else. Yet, I now had the bug or disease or whatever it is and was wishing another boy would take a dating interest in me.

With some encouragement and help from others, I finally was able to use the steps at school and on March 24, 1953, went up to the main floor. The ramp was hard and the 28 stairs were tiring. Gee, I can't express how wonderful it was to see more of the school, more of the kids, and finally be in another class. Of course, I felt cheated when I discovered there were only five boys in the English class. Oh well!

Since April, Daddy had started to teach me how to drive. He would take me down the lonely roads. I would use my right leg on the gas as we all do, but would have to use my left leg on the brake as I never regained the ability to move my right leg to the left. I passed the driver's license test that following August, but only with a letter from my doctor, explaining my need to use both legs to drive.

The remainder of the school year was very busy. I was asked to participate in a commercial typing contest in Provo, play piano in the Women's Federated Music Clubs Festival, and play background music for the school fashion show, in which a coat I had made was modeled by another student. I also was asked to play piano for many different occasions, recitals and festivals, for church or to accompany a chorus or individuals. I hardly had time to practice walking with only one cane. I kept practicing but just couldn't do it.

Only two and one half weeks left of school! I wished there were four months or more. I was just getting into it when it would soon be over. I was now going out to school three days a week and had finally been to my first school assembly the middle of May. I remember thinking the end of May just before graduation, "this is the last time I will be in a high school class and it just began!" I made an effort those last few days to personally thank the teachers and staff who had been so good to me the past few years. I successfully graduated from Spanish Fork High School in May 1955.

That summer I was offered a job by Richard Taylor, a lawyer in town. I really wanted to go to college but didn't want to go until I could go more independently. I finally got to the point that I could walk with one cane in the house because there were objects close by to support me if needed. I simply couldn't go outside with just my cane because I would sway to the side and I couldn't gain control of my balance.

Often people would comment on the way I had been cheerful, through all my illnesses. They thought that I showed myself cheerful whether I was or wasn't. They were wrong. It's just that I always felt cheerful or happy mostly when people were around. When I felt opposite, I took it out on my parents. I guess the Lord just meant for me to feel happy when I was around people. I didn't feel bitter towards anyone or anything. I didn't see why others should either.

The muscle transplant surgeries were what gave me the ability to eventually walk short distances with only one cane, use some stairs, drive a car, and more easily transfer and maneuver in a variety of situations. Dr. Clegg later told me that he carried my transplant surgery file with him throughout the remainder of his career, sharing our success with numerous other polio doctors and patients. I am forever grateful for his dedication to being a great doctor and finding new ways to make life better for so many of us polio survivors.

EPILOGUE

The Years That Followed

Through her indomitable spirit of persistence and endless positive attitude, Myrna eventually learned to walk short distances with one cane and longer distances with two canes or the arm of someone, balancing herself and throwing her legs forward like a pendulum.

As mentioned, after graduating from high school, Myrna worked for a year for Richard Taylor, a local attorney-at-law in Spanish Fork. That year, her friend Janet convinced her that she could go to college with the help of her and other friends who were already doing so. She offered help by giving Myrna an arm to walk between classes on the large campus. With her encouragement and faithful support, Myrna was able to study at Brigham Young University (BYU) and even live on campus and experience the social part of university life. They didn't take the same classes, but they were able to arrange their schedules so Janet could run from her class to Myrna's classroom and help her walk to her next class. In subsequent years, other roommates and friends also helped her get around campus. She graduated from BYU with a degree in Business Management and Accounting.

Myrna's graduation from BYU

Myrna then moved to Salt Lake City where she got a job with Fabian Clendenin Law firm as a legal secretary, bookkeeper and office manager.

Myrna working at the Salt Lake law firm

She also participated in the Salt Lake Chorale and taught some business classes at the LDS Business College. Making the most of her regained physical strength from the surgeries received and her continued efforts at keeping muscles strong, she traveled to 18 European countries, Canada, Mexico, and many US states with friends or family.

Upon arrival in Madrid with her dear friend Nadeane assisting

She met her husband Ralph Leo Thacker of Heber City, Utah in the summer of 1965 and they were married in the Salt Lake Temple in June of 1966. Over the next 7 years they had three children, Merrilee, Bryan and Randall.

Myrna's marriage to Ralph in 1966

Each child brought great joy and also new challenges to learn from and accept. Merrilee had significant learning disabilities, Bryan was born with a severe intellectual handicap, and Randall ended up being gay. She accepted each child as they were and worked tirelessly to provide unconditional love and to help them blossom in their own unique ways. She provided dedicated and loving care for 8 years to her mother who had Dementia, and 12 years to her husband who had Parkinson's Disease. She saw each new challenge as a teacher and sought answers, solutions, and the path forward through practical study and faith. As she said, "you can grow into anything."

Myrna, her husband and children

She served on the Learning Disabilities Board of Utah, actively lobbying at the Utah State Capitol for legislation and funding to support more inclusive learning for the disabled and published their monthly newsletter. She served as a Spiritual Living teacher, pianist and in other roles in The Church of Jesus Christ of Latter-Day Saints.

Many have described Myrna as a person of complete unconditional love, never judging another, always opening her doors especially to those different from her. Myrna's listening skills helped many family and friends through difficult times.

In many ways, you could say that she had a very 'normal' life with all that she accomplished – completing college, having a career, marrying, building a home, and having children. Yet, life was never the same after having polio. And, it came back to haunt her in her 40s when she began to suffer from the effects of Post-Polio Syndrome, eventually forcing her to use an automatic wheelchair at the age of 50.

1987 news article explaining Post-Polio Syndrome

Post-Polio Syndrome is a condition that affects polio survivors many years after recovery from an initial acute attack of the poliomyelitis virus. Survivors experience gradual new weakening in muscles that were previously affected by the polio infection. For Myrna, she lost the strength in her upper body and back and was unable to continue using canes. She also experienced very high levels of pain and fatigue during the last 30 years of her life. Yet, she never lost her spunk and drive to continue doing as much as she could to enjoy life, her family and friends.

Myrna in her wheelchair in 2013, excited for her vacation adventures

Myrna eventually lost the ability to transfer herself to her wheelchair in the summer of 2015 and became dependent on a Hoyer lift and the help of her children and professional caregivers. Her son Randall recalls the day she finally ended therapy efforts to keep her strength to transfer. Myrna responded to Randall's wondering if there was something else that could be done, by saying, "It's gone Randall. I've accepted it." Myrna lived another 9 months, finding joy in the small and simple things of life.

Myrna smiling in her Hoyer lift during her final year of life

She died, surrounded by her close family, at the age of 78 of respiratory failure due to complications related to Post-Polio Syndrome. It became clear during the last five years of her life that her lungs had been initially affected by polio as she repeatedly contracted pneumonia and also required oxygen to improve her sleep.

The effects of polio never went away for Myrna. They were there every single day. They were something she had to negotiate with when making decisions about how to use her limited energy and mobility. Prioritizing the most important things in life became paramount.

We can learn a lot from Myrna about what matters most—family, friends, service, humor, positive attitude, faith, acceptance, and never giving up.

ABOUT THE BOOK

Myrna was a vivacious and active youth who at the age of 14 was paralyzed from her waist down by polio in 1951. This is an inspiring story of how faith, positive attitude, persistence, and the unconditional love and support of family and a community led to her miraculous recovery from polio.

Made in the USA
Columbia, SC
17 December 2020